THE YOUNG MARIA CALLAS

This book was made possible through the support of the Istituto Italiano di Cultura/Italian Government Cultural Institute (IIC) of Los Angeles, Francesca Valente, Director; IIC San Francisco, Amelia Carpenito Antonucci, Director; IIC Washington, Rita Venturelli, Director; IIC New York, Riccardo Viale, Director; IIC Chicago, Annunziata Cervone, Director.

THE YOUNG MARIA CALLAS

EDITED BY BRUNO TOSI

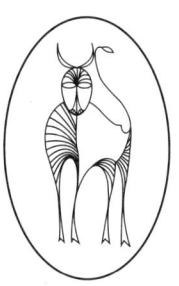

GUERNICA

TORONTO — BUFFALO — LANCASTER (U.K.)

2010

Original title: *Giovane Callas* (Maria Callas, Associazione culturale, Italia, 1997, 2007)
Translation by Bruno Tosi in collaboration with William Weaver,
Francis Keeping, Richard Barker and Anita Pensotti.
Copyright © 2010, by the Authors, Translators and Editors, and Guernica Editions.
Translation © 2010, by Bruno Tosi, William Weaver Estate, Francis Keeping, and Richard Barker.
All rights reserved. The use of any part of this publication, reproduced, transmitted in any form or by any means, electronic, mechanical, photocopying, recording or otherwise stored in a retrieval system, without the prior consent of the publisher is an infringement of the copyright law.

Antonio D'Alfonso, editor
Guernica Editions Inc.
P.O. Box 117, Station P, Toronto (ON), Canada M5S 2S6
2250 Military Road, Tonawanda, N.Y. 14150-6000 U.S.A.

Distributors:
University of Toronto Press Distribution,
5201 Dufferin Street, Toronto (ON), Canada M3H 5T8
Gazelle Book Services, White Cross Mills, High Town, Lancaster LA1 4XS U.K.

First edition.
Printed in Canada.

Legal Deposit – First Quarter
Library of Congress Catalog Card Number: 2010922927
Library and Archives Canada Cataloguing in Publication
Callas, Maria, 1923-1977
The young Maria Callas / Maria Callas ;
Bruno Tosi, editor. — 1st ed.
(Essay ; 57)
ISBN 978-1-55071-327-5
1. Callas, Maria, 1923-1977. 2. Sopranos (Singers) — Biography.
I. Tosi, Bruno II. Title. III. Series: Essay series (Toronto, Ont.) ; 57
ML420.C18A3 2010   782.1092   C2010-901306-9

CONTENTS

Introduction by Bruno Tosi 7
My First Thirty Years: The Memoirs of Maria Callas 11
Remembering Callas by William Weaver 58
From Florence into History by Alfredo Mandelli 84
The Memoirs of a Venetian Friend by Pucci Anfodillo 90
Maria Callas by Anita Pensotti 93
Seven Years with Maria by Pia Meneghini 102
The Young Callas by Bruno Tosi 124
The Voice of the Young Callas by Mario Merigo 170
Afterword by Francesca Valente 175
Chronology 177
Photo credits 183

TRANSLATOR'S NOTE

As this is a translation of recorded spoken recollections and articles written by people who were in some way close to Maria Callas and bearing in mind that the authors, for the most part, are not journalists or writers, I have taken into account the personal nature and style of their writing, maintaining the spelling of names and places and other irregularities as proposed by each contributor.

INTRODUCTION

Bruno Tosi

Over the last few years, more than a hundred books have been written about Maria Callas. Why a new book dedicated to the *La Divina?* Two thousand and seven marked the thirtieth anniversary of her death, on September 16, 1977 in Paris. It would seem that she chose to end the final act of this human drama that for her had ceased to have meaning. Her legend will never die. Nineteen-ninety-seven also marked the fiftieth anniversary of her Italian debut in the legendary *Gioconda* that took place on August 2, 1947 at the Arena of Verona. Later that year on December 30 she sang *Isolde* at the Fenice in Venice, the first hint of what she was to become.

At last the young Callas was being noticed. She had started her career at the age of fifteen singing in *Cavalleria Rusticana* in Greece during the Second World War. Her intensive period of activity (1939-1945) seems to me to have been of little use in the construction of an international career. However, her encounter with Elvira De Hidalgo was to be a crucial influence on her development as an artist. Although her subsequent three years in America were futile and resulted in no engagements, she did however meet the tenor Giovanni Zenatello and her colleague the bass Nicola Rossi Lemeni through Maestro

Sergio Failoni. After the non-event of the Chicago *Turandot*, she received a contract for the Verona *Gioconda*.

Here, Maria Callas first received international acknowledgement. It was at this time that she met other people who were to have a profound effect on both her career and her personal life: the distinguished conductor Tullio Serafin, the voice teacher Ferruccio Cusinati, the Pomari family and her future husband Giovanni Battista Meneghini with his sister Pia Meneghini. Francesco Siciliani, whom she also met at this time, was perhaps her real Pygmalion. He launched her at the Maggio Musicale in Florence in the repertoire for which she became famous. Last but not least, her little known encounter with Arturo Toscanini who, after a rather uncertain *Aida* in 1950 in which she replaced Renata Tebaldi, finally paved the way for the opening of the doors to La Scala. Milanese society opened its doors to her with the influence of Luchino Visconti. The transformation of Callas from a hefty American girl to a slim, charming and sophisticated diva is believed to be all their doing. This book concludes with her meeting Toscanini and her entrance into La Scala where so many triumphs awaited.

It is dedicated to the young Maria Callas: Maria, the child-prodigy, winner of radio contests in New York, her studies (in a detailed report) in Greece with Maria Trivella and the great Elvira De Hidalgo, her encounters after her arrival in Italy, in particular the years in Verona. The delightful non-edited draft by Anita Pensotti of the memoirs of Maria Callas written in 1957 for the weekly periodical OGGI and never again reproduced (thus constituting an unpublished work) is the most reliable source, taking into account that the singer, by this time at the peak of her fame both as a singer and socialite, watered down a few of the anecdotes and stories. Pensotti herself intervenes, detailing the context in which the episodes occurred.

Of great interest also, are the memoirs of Pia Meneghini, who for seven years was the tireless friend, counselor and companion to Maria Callas. She convinced her brother to marry Callas and organized the wedding, which was attended by only a few intimate friends. Pia Meneghini also reveals the secret of Callas' weight loss.

The story that follows tells us about the early career of the young Callas and runs parallel to that of Callas in her own words and those of her sister-in-law, incorporating where possible the various milestones along the way.

MY FIRST THIRTY YEARS

The Memoirs

Maria Callas

I

I have lately been asked many times by Italian and foreign journals, among them the American magazines *Time* and *Life*, to publish my memoirs. I have always refused. First of all because memoirs are usually written when one is advanced in years or when, presumably, one will have nothing more to say. In the second place – excuse me for saying this – I have not accepted because of my reticence. I hate talking about myself, so much so that I have always declined every proposal for reminiscences about my trips in order to avoid, which would have been impossible, any allusions to my success, always allowing others to speak at my expense, convinced that I was dealing with intelligent, kind, and generous people. Unfortunately, however, by dint of allowing others to speak, I find myself at the centre of innumerable rumors that are circling the globe. It is frankly in order to correct so many inaccuracies that I have made up my mind now, although reluctantly, to clear up the most important points of my private life and of my career as an artist. This story, therefore, has no polemical pretext, much less – God help me – any polemical intent. This story begs to be followed in the same spirit in which I have dictated it.

Let's begin then with my birth, as is obligatory in any biography. I came into the world in New York, under the sign of Sagittarius, the morning of the second or fourth of December. I cannot be precise with regard to this circumstance, as I am in all things concerning me, since my passport shows the date of birth as the second, while my mother maintains that she brought me into the world on the fourth. You choose the date you prefer. I prefer the fourth of December, first, because I have to believe what my mother says. Second, it's Saint Barbara's Day, the patroness of the artillery, a proud and combative saint whom I like in a special way. The year: 1923. The place: a clinic on Fifth Avenue, that is, right in the heart of New York and not in Brooklyn, where, I don't know why, certain journalists want at any cost to have me born. Not that there's anything ugly or shameful in the fact of being born in Brooklyn (I believe that that section was the birthplace of many famous people), but purely out of a love of accuracy.

I was registered at the Hall of Records as Maria Anna Cecilio Sophia Kalogeropoulos. My parents are both Greek: my mother, Evangelia Dimitriadu, who comes from a family of soldiers, is from Stilida, in the north of Greece, while my father is the son of farmers and he is a native of Meligala, in the Peloponnesus. After their marriage they took up residence in Meligala, where my father had a prospering pharmacy. They probably would not even have moved from there if they had not had the great sorrow of losing their only son, Vasily, at just three years of age. From that moment my father began to become intolerant, to want to distance himself as much as possible from the place where his son had died, and gradually the decision to move to America matured in him. They left in August 1923, four months before my birth, taking with them Jackie, my older sister, who was then six years old.

In New York, too, my father opened a very lovely pharmacy, and at the beginning everything went well. The business prospered, and we lived in an elegant apartment in the centre of town. Then came the terrible crisis of 1929, which shook our family too; the pharmacy was sold, and from that time on my father was little aided by good fortune. I should add that perhaps he is too honest and too much a gentleman to succeed in elbowing his way into the business jungle. Moreover, he has always been troubled by poor health. He now works as a pharmacist in hospital in New York and has a good position. He wouldn't leave America for anything, because he's lived there for thirty-four years and has become perfectly accustomed to it; but during my Mexico City and Chicago tours I always took him with me (my mother came with us once, too), and I had the joy of seeing him every evening in the theatre, seated beside my husband, while I sang.

Turning to my childhood, I have no particular recollection, except the vague intuition that my parents were not suited to each other. In fact, they now live apart, a thing that grieves me very much.

As for my vocation, there were never any doubts. My father tells of how I sang while still in the cradle, hurling vocalises and high notes so unusual for an infant that even the neighbors were stupefied. My mother's family, by the way, always boasted of an aptitude for singing. My grandfather had a magnificent dramatic tenor, but he was a career officer and understandably never thought of cultivating it. We're not speaking, though, of women. It would have been a scandal, an unbearable dishonor, to have a woman of the stage in the family. My mother, however, was of a different mind, and as soon as she became aware of my vocal gift decided to make me a child prodigy as quickly as possible. And child prodigies never have genuine childhoods. It's not a special toy that I remember – a doll or a favourite game – but, rather, the songs that I had to rehearse again and again, to the point of exhaustion, for the final test at the end of the school year; and above all the painful sensation of panic that overcame me when, in the middle of a difficult passage, it seemed to me that I was about to choke, and I thought, in terror, that no sound would emerge from my throat, which had become parched and dry. No one was aware of my sudden distress because, in appearance, I was extremely calm and continued to sing.

After grade school all my companions enrolled in high school or in secondary school, and I would very much have liked to follow their example, to become a high school student. But I couldn't: my mother had decided that I should not steal even a moment from a day spent in studying singing and piano. So, at eleven years of age, I put my books aside and began to get to know the enervating anxiety and the waiting involved in contests for child prodigies: I was regularly entered in them, for radio contests or for scholarship competitions. I always studied thanks to the scholarship, because after 1929 we were far from rich, and also because I was always full of pessimism about my possibilities. Even now, though I am charged with being conceited, I never feel secure about myself and torment myself with doubts and fears. Even as a child I didn't like the middle way: my mother wanted me to become a singer and I was quite happy to second her, but only on the condition that I be able one day to become a *great* singer. All or nothing: I certainly haven't changed in that regard with the passing of the years. The fact, therefore, of winning scholarships represented for me a firm guarantee that my parents were not deluded in believing in my voice. Comforted by that, I continued studying voice and piano with a kind of fury.

Toward the end of 1936 my mother wanted to return to Greece to see her family and to take Jackie and me with her.

My sister set out on her own somewhat before us; we were reunited in January or February 1937. In America, for ease of pronunciation, my father had shortened our last name, keeping only the first part and changing Kalous to Callas, two more harmonious syllables. I don't know whether he did that for any special reasons, but I remember that at school, too, I was regularly called Mary Callas. In Greece, on the other hand, I again became Maria Kalogeropoulos. When I arrived in Athens I had barely turned thirteen, but I looked older because I was as tall as I am now, stout, and altogether too serious, in my face and clothing, for my young age. My mother tried first to enrol me in the Athens Conservatory, the most important one in all of Greece; but they laughed in her face. What were they to make – they said – out of a thirteen-year-old girl? So, claiming to be sixteen, I entered another conservatory, the National, where I began studying with a teacher, probably of Italian origin, Maria Trivella. Barely a year later, however, I succeeded in achieving my aim and moved on, after a test that I passed brilliantly, to the Athens Conservatory, where I was entrusted to the wonderful teacher who had an essential role in my artistic formation: Elvira De Hidalgo.

It is to this illustrious Spanish artist, whom the public and the old subscribers at La Scala will certainly recall as an unforgettable and superlative Rosina and as a splendid interpreter of other very important roles, it is to this illustrious artist, I repeat, with a moved, devoted, and grateful heart, that I owe all my preparation and my artistic formation as an actress and musician. This elect woman, who, besides giving me her precious teaching, gave me her whole heart as well, was a witness to my whole life in Athens, including both my art and my family. She could say more about me than any other person, because with her, more than with anyone else, I had contact and familiarity. She tells the story of how I turned up for my lesson every morning at ten and stayed to hear all the other lessons, until six in the evening. If I know such a vast operatic repertory, I perhaps owe that precisely to that thirst for advice and instruction of which I wasn't even aware then. At the time, in October or November 1938, or eighteen years ago, my stage debut took place. For the first time, at less than fifteen years of age, I faced the footlights in the authoritative garb of the prima donna. My role was that of Santuzza in *Cavalleria Rusticana*, and everything went very well. But I was in despair because my face was swollen and contorted by a tremendous toothache. It has always been like that, at every important turn in my career. As you will see in the rest of the story of my life, I have always had to pay for all my triumphs immediately without fail, personally, with a sorrow or a physical ailment. That first success, however, opened the way for me to other auditions, and a few months later I was chosen to sing the part of Beatrice in the operetta *Boccaccio* at the Royal Opera House of Athens.

I remember that at that period my only preoccupation was my hands. I never knew where to put them: they seemed useless and cumbersome. My teacher, however, bemoaned my incredible clothes – and now I understand that she had a thousand reasons for doing so. Once, after having entreated me insistently to put on my most chic outfit, because she was going to introduce me to an important person, she saw me turn up in a dark red skirt, a blouse another shade of red – gaudy and strident – and on my head, atop rolled up braids, I had a ghastly hat of the Musetta type. I thought myself quite elegant and was very crestfallen when Madame Elvira tore off that absurd headgear, yelling that she would not give me any more lessons if I didn't make up my mind to improve my appearance. To tell the truth, even as it was I didn't know my looks. My mother was the one who thought about selecting my clothes, and she didn't allow me to stay in front of the mirror for more than five minutes. I had to study, I couldn't waste the time with nonsense, and certainly I owe it to her strictness that now, at just thirty-three, I have vast and extensive artistic experience. But on the other hand, I was deprived entirely of the joys of adolescence and of its innocent pleasures, those that are fresh, naive, and irreplaceable. I forgot to say that, by way of compensation, I got fat. Using the excuse that in order to sing well one needs to be hefty and blooming, I stuffed myself, morning and night, with pasta, chocolate, bread and butter, and zabaglione. I was rotund and rosy, with a quantity of pimples that drove me mad.

But let's continue in order. After *Boccaccio* the director of the Royal Opera House chose me again, for *Tosca*. The rehearsals lasted more than three months, without interruption, and I got so tired that even today that opera occupies the last place on my scale of preference. And so we arrive at the most painful period of my life, the very, very sad war years, of which I don't like to speak even with the people closest to me, so as not to irritate wounds that have not yet healed. I remember the winter of 1941. Greece was invaded by the Germans; the population had already been reduced to starvation for several months. It had never been so cold in Athens: for the first time in twenty years the Athenians saw snow. We were rehearsing d'Albert's *Tiefland*, the opera that is considered the German *Cavalleria*, and because of the fear of bombing we had to perform in a semidarkness that was diffused by acetylene lamps. For the whole summer I had eaten only tomatoes and boiled cabbage leaves, which I managed to obtain by covering kilometre after kilometre on foot and begging the farmers in the neighboring countryside to spare me a few of their vegetables. For those poor people a basket of tomatoes or some cabbage leaves could mean execution, because the Germans were implacable; nevertheless, I never returned empty handed. But in the winter of 1941 a friend of the family, then engaged to my sister, brought us a little cask of oil, corn flour, and potatoes; and I can't forget the incredulous stupefaction with which my mother, Jackie, and I looked at those precious goods, almost fearing that through witchcraft they could disappear at any moment.

No one who has not experienced the miseries of occupation and starvation can know what liberty and a tranquil and comfortable existence mean. For all the rest of my life I will never be able to spend money needlessly and will suffer – it's stronger than I am – at the waste of food, even if it's a bit of bread, a piece of fruit, or a little bit of chocolate. Later on, when the Italians came, we began to live a little better. His pity stirred by my progressive emaciation, a man who admired my voice, the owner of a butcher shop requisitioned by the invaders, introduced me to the Italian official in charge of distributing provisions to the troops. Once a month, for a paltry sum, he sold me ten kilos of meat, and I strapped the package to my shoulders and walked for an hour under the sun, even in the hottest months, as lightly and happily as if I were carrying flowers. That meat, in fact, was our greatest resource. We didn't have a refrigerator and so we couldn't keep it. But it was resold to our neighbors and with the proceeds we could get along by acquiring indispensable things.

Later the Italians "requisitioned" a group of opera singers, of which I was a part, for some concerts, and in accordance with our request they gave us provisions instead of money. Finally, after about a year, I was able to eat rice and pasta again and to drink good milk. In essence, the Italians were always good to me. At that time Madame De Hidalgo insisted that I learn Italian. "It will be useful for you," she would repeat, because sooner or later you will go to Italy. Only there will you be able to begin your real career. And in order to interpret and express well, you must know the exact meaning of every word. I listened to her and I tried not to allow myself to be charmed. Italy and La Scala represented an impossible dream for me, as though I might find myself on Mars or on the moon, and I rejected them even at the back of my mind so as to avoid delusions. Nevertheless, I bet my teacher that in three months I would manage to converse in Italian with her. But I didn't know how to do it. I certainly couldn't go to the head office of the fascists, as some people suggested I do, because my compatriots naturally would have considered me a traitor. I couldn't manage the money for private lessons. At that time I had struck up a friendship with four young doctors who had studied in Italy, and I don't know how, perhaps because I immediately liked the language of Dante enormously, but within three months I had won my bet.

In the summer of 1941, I had my first scrapes with colleagues. They were going to put on *Fidelio* and another prima donna had put herself out a great deal to get the part and had succeeded in getting it, but she was too busy to learn it. Since the rehearsal had to begin immediately, I was asked whether I could replace her, and I naturally accepted, because I knew the score to perfection. I'm telling you this episode in order to show that my only weapon – a very powerful and fair one – is always to be prepared, because nothing holds up against bravery. On the stage, before the curtain rises, the only thing that speaks is courage. They say that I always win. These are my means: work and preparation. If you consider those means harsh, then I really don't know what to say.

Immediately after the performance of *Fidelio*, which was given in the marvellous amphitheatre of Herodes Atticus, came the liberation, and then the attacks began against me on the part of my colleagues. But we will speak of them again later. In the meantime, finally, the administration of the Royal Opera

House granted me three months of vacation, and my mother, without losing any time, immediately found a job for me at the British headquarters, where I was assigned to the office of distribution of secret mail. We started work at eight, but I had to get up at six thirty because in order to save money I made the whole trip on foot, and our house, at 61 Patissiou, was very far from the office. The British offered us an abundant noon meal, and rather than taking it at headquarters, I had it put in a pot and carried it home to share with my mother. (At that time my sister Jackie wasn't living with us). I had a break for an hour and a half in all, so I had a quarter of an hour, more or less, at home. I went on like that until the winter: but even now, when I'm well, I feel the effects of the exhaustion that was left to me, like a sad inheritance, by a liver complaint and blood pressure reading of 90 at the most.

Excuse the digression and let us continue. We are at 1945: the time had come to renew my contract with the Royal Opera House, but I found out from a maternal uncle, a doctor at the Royal House (Professor Constantine Louros), that Ralis, then the head of the Greek government, had received my colleagues en masse. They had gone to protest to him, threatening a full-dress strike in the event that I was again engaged as a prima donna at the Royal Opera House. It was a disgrace, they railed, that a girl of twenty-one be compared to artist of their talent and their age. My uncle didn't know what to advise me, but since there's always a beneficent God to help those who travel the straight and narrow and never do any harm to anyone, when I least expected it, the American Consulate offered me a ticket to America. I would repay the money, I was told, when I could.

The director of the Royal Opera House was very embarrassed when he had me summoned to explain to me that I would no longer be engaged as a prima donna. I allowed him to stammer out a bunch of excuses, then announced to him that I was leaving for America, adding, Let's hope that you won't have to regret this one day. But before departing I wanted to give a last sample of my skills and I sang Millöcker's *The Beggar Student*, an operetta as difficult as anything for a soprano: they were obliged to entrust it to me because no one else could sing it.

I left on the *Stockholm* (the ship that collided with the *Andrea Doria* last July). I hadn't written my father that I would be arriving: my mother had advised against it: I don't know why. Or perhaps I do, but there's no need for me to state it. I took three or four dresses with me and didn't have a cent in my pocket. My mother and my sister refused to accompany me to Piraeus: they said they would not, be able to stand the commotion. On the other hand, some friends came, among them the tuberculosis specialist Papatesta, who lived in the apartment below ours.

They gave me a farewell dinner. I remember very well: it was two in the afternoon. A few minutes before embarkation I was fervently advised: Be careful and don't lose your money. Where have you put it? There's no danger, I replied, I don't have any. They couldn't believe me. They took my pocketbook, turned it inside out, and didn't find anything. The *Stockholm* was to leave Piraeus at three, and at that hour the banks were closed. None of them could help me, but I waved to them happily. I was going to meet the unknown; nevertheless, at that moment I felt with extraordinary clarity that I need not be afraid.

2

At twenty-one, alone and without a cent, I boarded a ship at Athens – as I've told you – headed for New York. Now, at a distance of twelve years, I realize exactly what grave consequences I could have encountered and what incredible risks I was facing in returning to America at the end of a world war, with the prospect of not being able to track down either my father or my old friends. But, as I said, I was not afraid; and it was not just a question of courage, or rather, the unawareness that was typical of my very young age. It was something deeper: an instinct, unlimited faith in the divine protection that – I was sure of that – would not fail me.

You will see for yourselves; as my story continues, how the hand of God has always been over my head – permit me this expression – at all the most dramatic moments of my life. I first experienced that when I was six years old. I was walking with my parents, and suddenly I saw Jackie, who was playing ball on the other side of the street, with our housekeeper and a cousin. It often happens with me – it's a characteristic side of my personality – that I'm seized by sudden tender impulses and feel ashamed of them immediately afterward, I don't know why, perhaps because of excessive modesty about my feelings. At that time, too, catching sight of my sister, I ran to her to give her a kiss and than ran away, red and embarrassed, precipitously crossing the street just at the moment when a car was coming along at great speed. I was knocked over and dragged to the end of the street. The American newspapers (that was the first time they took an interest in me) called me lucky Maria on that occasion, because I managed to recover in almost miraculous fashion, after being unconscious for twelve days and when everyone, from the chief physician to the janitor at the hospital, considered me a hopeless case.

I have good reason to say that I also merited the appellation lucky Maria in another very grave hour of my life, which goes back to the Greek period. On December 4, 1944 – I remember it very well because it was my birthday – civil war erupted in Athens. As I have said, I was then working for the British Command and my superiors recommended that I shouldn't leave headquarters, because, having occupied such a delicate post as that of distribution of secret mail, I would undoubtedly be a victim of communist reprisals and subjected to inevitable torture. But our house was located in the zone occupied by the Reds, and I didn't want to leave my mother on her own. For that reason I had myself taken, in a jeep, to Patissiou Street, and for several days I stayed locked in my room. I was racked with fear; moreover, I was sick thanks to a box of very old beans that, for the lack of anything else, I had decided to eat (and by the way, I have a real and genuine allergy to every kind of dry legume). In that condition I couldn't even think of procuring provisions for my mother and myself, and I might have died of starvation (many people died of it at the time) if I hadn't had the help of my friend Doctor Papatesta, who brought me some of the little food that he had at his disposal.

At a certain moment I received a visit from a pale and poorly dressed boy – he looked like a coal vender – who asserted that he had been charged with a mission concerning me by an official of the British Command. Terrified, suspecting a trap, I tried to chase him away in a rude manner; then, since his insistence had become unbearable, I resigned myself to listening to him. He was in reality a secret agent whom the British had sent to beg me to return to headquarters, because they feared for my life and were amazed that the communists had not yet arrested me. The fellow found it very hard to convince me; but at last he persuaded me that it was absolutely essential for me to go back to the British zone, and without wasting time I called Doctor Papatesta to entrust my mother to him.

Our house (my mother and sister still live there) is on a beautiful, very spacious and tranquil avenue, that comes out on Concord Square. But when I think of that avenue I always see it in my imagination as I saw it that morning, literally covered with broken glass and all sorts of wreckage that had fallen out of windows as a result of the constant machine gun fire: gray and silent. A tremendous, unnerving silence that would last sixty seconds, to be broken, once a minute, by the communists' terrible "blind volley," shots at regular intervals that could hit anyone and had the specific aim of wearing down the populace's nerves. Even now I can't explain to myself how I could have run desperately through the midst of that devastation, under fire, and arrive safe and sound at the British headquarters.

I've told this episode only to show – and you will hear me repeat this often – that the good Lord has always helped me. Do you know, in fact – to pick up the thread of the conversation – whom I found waiting for me when I disembarked in New York? Precisely the person whom I would have least expected: my father, who had learned of my arrival from one of the Greek-language newspapers that are published in America. I really don't know how to describe the limitless relief with which I drew myself to him, hugging him as though he had been raised from the dead, and crying on his shoulder from joy.

I've already had occasion to tell you that my father is hardly rich; but in that year and half that I lived with him he treated me like a queen, making up for everything that I had suffered. He got a new, very pretty bedroom set for me, clothes, and elegant shoes. I was happy and was beginning little by little to regain faith in myself, because every time that a Greek ship dropped anchor in port, sailors or officers turned up at our house, wanting to greet the famous singer Maria Kalogeropoulos. And they told my father that many of them, at the time of *Fidelio*, made their way on foot from Piraeus to the Acropolis (a preposterous thing, if you know Athens), braving the German roundups, simply in order to hear me sing. Their words did me good: in those years, as you have seen, I thought only of studying and of earning a living, taking advantage of the natural gift of my voice, without even realizing that in the meantime fame and the public's favor had risen around my name.

Comforted by the evidence, I decided, with courage, to win a place for myself in New York. In the final analysis, I told myself, I was a singer who had seven years of an intense career behind her. I hoped, ingenuously, to find some engagements. But who in America knows poor little Greece? And who can lend an ear to a twenty-one-year-old girl? I realized very quickly, with bitterness, that I would have to start all over again from the beginning.

At that time, not having much to do, I often went to the pharmacy where my father worked; and there one morning the owner of the store introduced me to an ex-singer who invited me to her home to hear her pupils and give my opinion of them. I spent three or four hours with her, every Saturday, and sometimes I helped, giving advice to her students. I remember that one of those Saturdays – it was getting close to Christmas – a Mr. Edward Bagarozy came to say hello to this ex-singer, his friend, to give her his greetings. I was invited to sing. After having listened to me attentively, Mr. Bagarozy proposed that I participate in the opera season that he intended to call the United States Opera Company. He promised that I would be the prima donna in *Turandot* and perhaps also in *Aida*.

Meanwhile, I had obtained an audition at the Metropolitan, but I could not agree with the administration because I was offered parts that I believe unsuited to my possibilities at that time, namely, *Fidelio* (which I didn't want to sing in English) and *Butterfly*, which I refused without hesitation. I was in fact convinced that I was a "fatty." In fact I weighed 176 pounds and 176 pounds is a lot, but not excessive for a tall woman like me, five feet eight inches. I had received other offers that I refused, and I was given a letter of introduction, by Elvira De Hidalgo, to Romano Romani, the maestro for the famous Rosa Ponselle. In response to my request for lessons, Maestro Romani said, "I don't see the necessity. You need above all and only to work." I was also heard by poor Maestro Merola, from San Francisco, who, after paying me a number of compliments, gave way to the usual tired refrain: "You're so young . . . what guarantee can I have . . . who will assure me! First," he concluded, "make a career in Italy, and then I'll sign you up." "Thank you," I replied, dejected and furious, "thank you very much, but when I've made my career in Italy, I'm certain that I will no longer have any need of you."

I remember very well that at that time I went from one movie house to another, not to see the films, but so as not to go out of my mind from torturous thoughts about my uncertain future. Then, finally, came the time when I was to sing *Turandot* with the United States Opera Company. But the season fell through for lack of funds. Among famous colleagues who suffered because of that were Galliano Masini (who was at the height of his popularity), Mafalda Favero, Cloe Eimo, the tenors Infantino and Scattolini, the baritone Danilo Checchi, Nicola Rossi-Lemeni, Max Lorenz, the Konetzki sisters, various artists of the Paris Opera, poor Maestro Failoni, and others whose names I don't recall.

In great haste they had to organize a concert to collect the money necessary for tickets home, and immediately afterward the Italian singers all returned to Italy. Rossi-Lemini remained in New York, attracted by vague promises of work. While waiting for better times, Nicola and I studied together at Bagarozy's apartment, because I didn't have a piano at my house, and it was Rossi-Lemini who told me one afternoon: "I've been signed up for this year's season at the Verona Arena, and I've heard that Giovanni Zenatello, the famous tenor, the director of the Arena, is having trouble finding a Gioconda to his taste. Do you want me to ask for an audition for you? He's staying here in New York, and the thing can be managed immediately." I said yes, of course.

At that time the name Verona had no meaning for me at all. I would never have been able to imagine that precisely in that city, which is now so dear to me, the most important events of my life would come to fruition. As I will relate later, in fact, I met my husband in Verona; I had my first Italian success in Verona; and I met Renata Tebaldi in Verona.

So I went to Zenatello and got a contract for *La Gioconda* with a fee of 40,000 lire per performance. Meanwhile, I knew that my mother and father were not swimming in money – in fact, they had to work hard just to get along. My mother had wanted to return to New York at all costs, and in order to be able to pay for the trip I had had to borrow the money from my godfather. Professor Leonidas Lantzonis, the assistant director of the Orthopedic Hospital of New York. When the time came for my departure for Italy, I was forced to turn to him again.

So there I was, having to take the sea route again, still poor as a church mouse (I had fifty dollars, all that my father could give me), but – it's appropriate to say – with an enormous baggage car of hopes and with the incredible joy of one who sees, almost with fear, an impossible dream coming true. I landed at Naples on June 29, 1947, where the heat was hellish. With me were Rossi-Lemini and Mrs. Louise Bagarozy,

Edward's wife, who intended to attempt a singing career in Italy. We left our trunks in Naples. They reached us later, after having become noticeably lighter during storage. We took the train to Verona. We found only one empty seat and took turns sitting there all night without managing to close our eyes, because the two who were standing didn't stop looking impatiently at their watches, waiting for their turn. On the very morning of my arrival in Verona I was met at the Hotel Academia (where a room had been taken for me) by my poor and very dear Gaetano Pomari, the assistant director of the Arena, and Giuseppe Gambato, the municipal secretary and a lover of the arts. They came to invite me to a dinner in my honor that was to take place following day. I went, of course, and there, twenty-four hours after setting foot on Italian soil, I shook the hand of my future husband, Giovanni Battista Meneghini.

Allow me to recount in all the details the meeting with my life's companion – a chapter that all women, after all, recall with extraordinary pleasure. At that time my husband shared a place with poor Pomari, because his apartment had been requisitioned during the war; and since he loved opera, he took a willing part in all the great discussions that precede every opening of the Verona season. The evening before my arrival he had asked jokingly: "And what task do you entrust to me for the production of *La Gioconda*? Let me take care of the ballerinas this time." "No," they replied, "you will take care of the prima donnas. The American one is arriving tomorrow, and we've been thinking of entrusting her to your care." Battista was very tired those days; the large brick factories of which he was director and co-owner took up his days entirely. When he left his office and the time came for him to participate in the dinner, he decided that, all in all, it would be better to go rest: he had to leave very early the next morning, as usual. As he was going up the stairs (the apartment was directly over the Pedavena, the restaurant where we were eating) he was overtaken by a waiter – a certain Gigotti, I still remember his name – who told him, in Veronese dialect, "Come downstairs, sir, or Mr. Pomari will be furious." Titta (that's what I call him) pretended not to have heard; but since the waiter insisted, after a few moments of hesitation – decisive ones for my life – he turned around and hurried down the stairs.

I remember that when we were introduced – he was dressed in white – I thought to myself: "This is a honest, sincere person. I like him." Then I forgot him, because he wasn't seated next to me at the table, and without my glasses (as is well known, I'm very nearsighted) I could make him out only obscurely. At a certain moment, however, Louise Bagarozy, who was beside me, passed on to me an invitation from Meneghini. Battista wanted to take her, Rossi-Lemini, and me to Venice the next morning. I agreed at once, but changed my mind the next day: my trunk had not yet arrived and the only dress I had was the one I was wearing. Rossi-Lemini, however, did so much and talked so much that he managed to persuade me. To conclude, I went to Venice with Battista, and during that trip our love was born at a single stroke.

I should say, at this point, that up to that time Titta had not yet heard me sing. That happened some twenty days later, when Maestro Serafin arrived from Rome. He – I was immensely proud of that – was to conduct *Gioconda*. The audition took place in the Adelaide Ristori Theater and went off in the best possible way. I was very happy, Serafin was enthusiastic, and Battista was even more enthusiastic.

But, as usual, during the dress rehearsal at the Arena, I had to pay the price of my success in hard cash. In the second act, in order not to run into the artificial sea surrounding the ship, I wound up in one of those entrances through which wild animals at one time exited. Fortunately, there was a wooden chute; otherwise I would have cracked my head on those rocks. I sprained my ankle, and instead of having it bandaged immediately, I chose to continue the rehearsal. (I often have these attacks of conscientiousness, which always end in harm for myself). At the end of the third act the ankle was so swollen that I couldn't even allow my foot to touch the ground. A doctor was called, but by then it was already too late, and because of the tremendous pain I didn't manage to close my eyes the whole night. I remember the gratitude and tenderness I felt that evening for Titta, who stayed by my bed until dawn, seated on a chair, to help me and comfort me.

That is just a little episode that shows the nature of my husband, for whom I would be willing to give my life, immediately and with joy: it was then I realized that I would never meet a man more generous than he and that God had been very good to me in placing him on my path. If Battista had wished, I would have abandoned my career without any regrets, because in a woman's life (I mean a real woman) love is more important, beyond compare, than any artistic triumph. And I sincerely wish anyone who lacks it a fourth or even a tenth of my conjugal happiness.

Let's return to *Gioconda*. I made my debut at the Arena, then, with a bandaged leg, was scarcely able to drag myself around that enormous stage. But I had completely recovered when, at Castelveccio, I attended a reception given in honor of all the singers of the Verona season. On that occasion I saw for the first time my dear colleague Renata Tebaldi, whom I have always admired and whom I still admire very much. Renata – that's what I called her at the time of our friendship, and I don't see any reason why I should alter that – had sung in *Faust*, and perhaps because of an involuntary oversight on the part of our hosts, she wasn't introduced to me during the party. But I haven't forgotten the agreeable impression made on me by that beautiful girl, by that wholesome, happy, and cordial face. I'll have to return to the topic of Renata many times in the instalments that follow.

3

After the performance of *Gioconda* at the Verona Arena, I deluded myself by thinking that I would obtain many engagements. On the contrary, I received a single offer, from the theatrical agent Liduino Bonardi, who offered me *Gioconda* at Vigevano. I refused; I was to regret that bitterly a short while later when finally, for lack of anything better, I decided to accept the offer and it was already too late: he had found someone else. Meanwhile, La Scala asked me to audition, and Maestro Labroca, then the artist director of the theatre, had me sing excerpts from *Norma* and *Ballo in Maschera*. Trembling, I waited for his evaluation and heard him say that my voice had too many defects. "Try to correct them," Labroca added, "and in a month I'll call for you. But return home calm. I assure you that you'll have the part of Amelia in *Ballo in Maschera*."

I waited a month, two months in vain (how many tears on Titta's shoulders); then the good Lord decided to help me again. One day Maestro Serafin decided to mount *Tristan* at the Fenice in Venice, and for the part of Isolde he thought of the young American singer whom he had conducted in *Gioconda* at Verona. He asked the director of the Fenice, Maestro Nino Cattozzo, to locate me, and Cattozzo telephoned a friend of my husband in Verona (I prefer to keep his name a secret) to have him furnish my address that very evening and to tell him whether I knew the part and was prepared to accept it. I, of course, knew nothing about any of this. But in the evening, guided by a sure presentiment, Battista advised me to go back to Liduino Bonardi the next day to find out whether there was any possibility of contracts for me. And whom did I find there as soon as I entered the agency? Maestro Cattozzo, who, not having received the desired response, had gone to Milan to look for another Isolde. "I'm happy to see you, he said, "Have you changed your mind?" "About what?" "But weren't you asked about *Tristan* at the Fenice?" I came down to earth and understood everything, with great sadness.

Cattozzo also told me that Serafin would come to Milan the next day for the audition and asked me whether I knew *Tristan*. Out of fear of losing the likely engagement I answered yes without hesitating, and when Serafin arrived in Milan I went to see him at the beautiful home of Carmen Scalvini, whom I was seeing for the first time and who was very nice to me. The rehearsal went well and the Maestro wanted to congratulate me, but I couldn't keep from confessing the truth to him, and that is that I had learned only a little of the first act of *Tristan*, and that had been a long time ago. Serafin wasn't frightened; he suggested that I go to Rome for a month to study the opera with him. That's what I did, and I signed a contract with the Fenice, a contract that included not only *Tristan* but *Turandot* as well. The fee, not without a certain effort, was raised: imagine, from the 40,000 at Verona to 50,000 per performance! No one protested at that time!

One evening, during the run of *Tristan*, while I was removing my makeup in my dressing room, I heard the door open, and in the doorway, all of sudden, was framed the tall figure of Tebaldi, who was in Venice to sing – I don't know if it was for the first time – *Traviata*, with Serafin. As I've already said, we knew each other only by sight, but this time we shook each other's hands warmly, and Renata gave me such spontaneous compliments that I was enchanted. "Good heavens!" she said, "if I had had to perform such an exhausting part, they would have had to pick me up with a spoon!" I think that very rarely, between two women of the same age and same profession, could there arise an attraction as fresh and immediate as that which was born between us. My attraction to her became authentic affection some time later, at Rovigo, where Tebaldi was singing in *Andrea Chenier* and I in *Aida*. At the end of the aria "O patria mia" I heard a voice from a box seat cry out, "Brava, brava Maria!" It was Renata's voice. From that time we became – I can well say so – dearest friends. We were often together, and we exchanged advice about clothes, hairdos, and even about repertory. Later, unfortunately, our schedules did not allow us to enjoy fully that friendship any longer. We met only in passing, between one trip or another, but always, I think, I'm even quite sure of it, with mutual pleasure. She admired my dramatic force and physical endurance; I, her very sweet singing. At this point I want to make it clear that if I so often followed her performances with attention, I did it exclusively in order to try to understand the quite special way in which Renata sings; and I'm infinitely sorry to hear such a ridiculous accusation levelled against me that I wanted to "intimidate" her. The public, Renata, and much more so the people with whom she surrounds herself, can't understand that I – and I'm by no means ashamed of this – always discovered something to learn from the voices of my colleagues, not just the famous ones like Tebaldi, but even from the humble and mediocre ones. Even the voice of the most modest student can offer instruction to us. And I, who torture myself, hour after hour in the exhausting search for continual improvement, will never be able to give up listening to colleagues sing.

Before entering into this long digression about Tebaldi, I was talking about my performance in *Tristan* and *Turandot* at the Fenice. Even though it's not for me to say so, I had a great success in both operas. Then I sang *Forza del Destino* in Trieste (where the critics who have to move on stage), *Turandot* at Verona, in Rome, at the Baths of Caracalla, and lastly, *Tristan* again, at Genoa, in May 1948. Often, when recalling that *Tristan* at Genoa, I laugh to the point of crying. Since the Carlo Felice Theater, seriously damaged by bombings, had not been restored, the opera was performed in the Grattacielo Theater, that is to say, in a movie house with a very tiny stage. Imagine the company that I was part of, with my plentiful 165 pounds (thirty-three more than now), Elena Nicolai, very tall and robust, Nicola Rossi-Lemini, also tall and robust, Max Lorentz, the same size, and the baritone Raimondo Torres, of no smaller size!

Image all these colossi moving around in a tiny, tiny little theatre, struggling with an opera that requires ample, solemn, and absolutely dramatic gestures! I remember that when as Isolde I ordered Nicolai (Brangane) to run to the prow of the ship to tell Tristan that I wished to speak with him, I couldn't manage to keep a straight face. In fact, not having any room, Elena could only move away slightly, at most two or three meters, and in order to allow the time expected for the stage action to pass, she kept pirouetting around, stirring up our hilarity. It was a stupendous performance, however, and the Genoese haven't forgotten it.

A few months later, while I was in Rome preparing *Norma* with Serafin, with which I was to inaugurate the season at the Communale in Florence, the first symptoms of appendicitis appeared. I decided not to pay any attention to those annoyances, but in December, during the opening performance of *Norma*, I realized that the cramps in my right leg were becoming more and more insistent, so much, so that kneeling cost me tremendous effort. I had to have an operation, giving up *Aida* in Florence, and for three or four days after the operation I had a temperature of 41 degrees centigrade [105 degrees Fahrenheit].

Battista feared for my life. I recovered rather quickly, but I was still convalescing when I threw myself, with my usual fury, into preparing *Walkyrie* for the Fenice in Venice. I want to clarify a specific notion of mine: one shouldn't confuse duty and ambition. Coming from a long theatrical career, I have learned this inexorable law to perfection: the show must go on, even if the protagonist dies. That's why I'm so tenacious in my work, only because it's a question of duty, not of ambition.

During that period of intense activity my greatest regret was being forced to be away from Titta too often. I often loathed my career because its requirements forced me to be apart from him, and I dreamed of abandoning it.

So we have arrived at January 1949. I was engaged in performances of *Walkyrie* in Venice, and I learned that Margherita Carosio had fallen ill with the flu and would not be able to sing *Puritani* (again, at the Fenice). I was in the lobby of the Hotel Regina, with Serafin's wife and daughter, and almost mechanically, on learning that news, I moved to the piano and began leafing through the score, reading at sight and ad-libbing a few arias. Mrs. Serafin sat up in her chair. "As soon as Tullio arrives," she said, "you'll sing that for him." Thinking that she was joking, I calmly said yes. But on the next day, at ten – I was sound asleep – I was awakened by the phone, again by Maestro Serafin, who ordered me to come downstairs immediately, without even washing my face, so as not to lose any time. I put on my dressing robe and went down half asleep, without realizing what was wanted of me. In the music room I found, beside Serafin, Maestro Cattozzo and a substitute maestro, who ordered me, almost in chorus, to sing the aria from *Puritani* that I had ad-libbed the night before. I looked at them with bewilderment. I swear that at that moment I suspected that they were mad. But then I surrendered, sang, and stayed to hear them propose to me right away, without batting an eyelash, that I prepare *Puritani* in order to replace Margherita Carosio. They were giving me six days and I didn't know the opera at all; in addition, I had performances of *Walkyrie*. It still seems incredible to me, but we managed it. That very day, Wednesday, I studied *Puritani* for several hours and sang *Walkyrie* in the evening; Thursday, several more hours of study; and again on Friday, with a performance of *Walkyrie* in the evening. Saturday afternoon, with a nervousness that I hope is understandable, I went through the first dress rehearsal of *Puritani*; the next day, the last matinee of *Walkyrie* and the dress rehearsal of *Puritani*.

Puritani went on stage punctually on Tuesday, with a happy outcome. Then I sang *Walkyrie* in Palermo, *Turandot* in Naples, *Parsifal* in Rome (I learned it in five days), and between one performance and another I took part in my first radio concert, at Turin, with the following program: the "Liebestod," "O patria mia," "Casta diva," and the aria from *Puritani*. I'm telling you this in perhaps excessive detail because I have often been accused by people, or rather by my adversaries, of wanting to sing everything: it was only chance and my friends' insistence, not my exaggerated ambition, that opened the way to such an unusual and rich repertory.

I have said that in spite of my growing success, I wasn't content. I wanted, in fact, the warmth of my own home and the tranquillity that every woman derives from a happy marriage. I would have married Titta the day I met him, but there is a distinct difference in age between my husband and me, and Titta, being the honest person that he is, didn't want to push me into a step that I might regret. He wanted me to be sure, to take time to think calmly, but at the beginning of 1949

I had thought enough. I was to leave in the spring for a round of performances in Buenos Aires, and I preferred to have Maria Menighini on my passport instead of Maria Callas.

So we decided to get married and began taking steps to obtain the necessary marriage documents. Since I'm an adherent of the Orthodox faith, I had to have the Vatican's approval, but a priest from Verona, Professor Mortari, assured Battista that once we had all the papers, we would be able to resolve that problem without any trouble. The Vatican posed no difficulties; in April my documents had arrived from New York and Athens in good order, and Titta's were also ready. My departure date was fixed for April 21, and there was no longer time to organize a wedding ceremony with lots of flowers, "Ave Maria," and a reception, as I would have liked. Therefore we decided to defer the wedding until August 15, my name day, when I would be back from Argentina. My husband, however, with the prudence characteristic of businessmen, wanted to have in his hands all the documents, which in the meantime had been taken to the Archbishopric for the certification of the marriage license, already obtained.

The morning of April 21st, a few hours before I left Verona, Battista sent his secretary to retrieve the documents. But at noon the woman, who was usually capable and businesslike, had not yet returned. When she finally appeared, her clouded face told us that unforeseen obstacles had turned up. She said, in fact, that at the Archbishopric she had been assured that the documents weren't ready; she then added that – it seemed to her – what must be in our way was some great difficulty interjected by the family. In reality it became known later that two individuals had taken the trouble to present themselves at the Archbishopric to whisper that it would be very appropriate, on the part of the religious authorities, to create insurmountable obstacles for the marriage. Neither my husband nor I wish to name the two because these are matters that concern only our families and their economic interest. In any event, Battista wasted no time. He told me (I received the news with enormous surprise and great joy) to be ready, because at three in the afternoon we would be married at Zevio, near Verona, at the town hall. Then he hurried to the Archbishopric, where, in sorrowful and firm tones, he asked Monsignor Zancanella to return all the papers to him because since we could not be wed in a church, we would be united in matrimony with just the civil rites.

His words apparently were sufficiently effective, and the prompt and considerate intervention of one of Titta's friends, Mario Orlandi, must have been equally effective. At five in the afternoon everything was ready for our wedding at the Church of the Philippines in Verona. Since I'm of the Orthodox faith, as I've said, the rite was celebrated in a side chapel. There were six of us in all: the priest, who spoke such moving words that I cried, the sacristan, two witnesses, and Titta and I. We exchanged vows and swore eternal love. I was dressed in blue, with black lace over my head. I hadn't had time to buy a new dress. The ceremony did not take long. Once again I had been deprived of the joys and fantasies dearest to the female heart: the wedding preparations, the gifts, the flowers.

No preparations, no gifts, no flowers. Only great love and an exalted simplicity. Immediately afterward I returned to the hotel and packed the trunk that would follow me to Buenos Aires. Titta accompanied me to Genoa, and the following morning, very sad and alone, I boarded the *Argentina*, headed for Buenos Aires.

4

During that lonely and melancholy trip aboard the *Argentina* I came down with the flu when we crossed the Equator, and it was five days before I managed to recover. For that reason the performances of *Turandot* and *Norma* at the Colon in Buenos Aires are linked in my memory to the prolonged effort that it cost me to rise from my bed, in spite of a temperature, and to arrive, by force of will, at the conclusion of the performance. The South American tour lasted until the middle of July and was a long period of torture for me because the public's enthusiasm could not compensate for my being away from Titta, the man whom I had married one afternoon three months earlier and whom I had had to abandon the day after the wedding.

I finally returned to Italy, to my husband, who in the meantime had furnished a cozy apartment above his firm's offices at 21 San Fermo, right behind the Arena. But the joy of living together was made bitter right from the very first days by many family troubles; troubles in which the motive of financial interest was fatally involved, which led, unfortunately, to interminable squabbles. I do not wish to linger, however, over this question, one that is too delicate and personal. In December of that same year, 1949, I opened, for the first time, the opera season at the San Carlo in Naples, with *Nabucco*; then I went to the Rome Opera for *Tristan* and at the same time accepted an offer for *Aida* in Brescia. I remember that Maestro Serafin didn't want me to submit to this *tour de force*, the more so as my *Aida* would be followed fifteen days later by that of Tebaldi's at La Scala. That coincidence, however, left me completely indifferent, and I saw no reason to withdraw from my contract with Brescia for such a futile reason. I therefore began shuttling – by train – between Brescia and the capital, and in exchange for this tremendous wear and tear I asked the

Milanese theatrical agency for a single favour: to get me the costumes and wigs that I had already worn many times before for performances of *Aida* and that I usually rented from a Florentine tailor's shop. I received the most fulsome promises, of course, but at the dress rehearsal the costumes hadn't arrived. Mrs. Scalvini, however, whom I hadn't seen in a long time, was there. She wanted to know the reason for my obvious worry and guaranteed – she was taking the responsibility upon herself, she said – that I would have costumes. But two evenings later, when I arrived at the theater for the opening performance, I found a piece of silk the colour of red brick, as long as my body, with a cut in the middle for the head and two seams at the sides. That is exactly how it was and I beg you not to think I'm exaggerating. And let's not talk about the wig, suitable at best for a baby. Furious – didn't I perhaps have reason to be? – I began yelling, and I screamed at Mrs. Scalvini, who just at that moment turned up in my dressing room, "What costumes have they given you. You've let them to put one over on you!"

The deplorable incident didn't manage to compromise the performance because, as always happens, desperation suggested a superb idea to me. At the last moment – the performance was already a half hour late in starting – I remembered that the singer who was playing Amneris (I think it was Pirazzini) had her own costume as well as the theater's. I tried on the latter and fortunately it fit well enough. Fortunately, moreover, I'm a brunette, not a blonde. Because of that I was able that evening, by gathering my hair into a thick bun, to perform Aida without the traditional wig. But the surprises weren't over. Immediately after the famous aria "O patria mia," at the moment when the audience was about to applaud, a voice from the gallery ordered, in Brescian dialect, "Quiet, the aria isn't finished." There were several seconds of perplexity in the orchestra, enough time, you understand, to deprive me of my applause. But every time that I'm the victim of an injustice – by now I know it from experience – I'm rewarded at the end with a true, warm triumph: and that was the case on this occasion, too. Nevertheless, I returned to Rome very regretful that, in my stubbornness, I had refused to follow Serafin's advice.

After *Tristan* I sang Norma in Roma and *Aida* again, in Naples. Then, in the company of my very dear colleague Giulietta Simionato, I left for a series of performances in Mexico, and it was a trip full of vicissitudes that nearly cost Giulietta her life. It is an episode about which I can now smile because of its happy outcome, but for a long time it came into my dreams like a terrible nightmare. We had arrived in New York, Simionato and I; the heat was awful, and we were exhausted from a stormy crossing. The plane for Mexico City that was supposed to leave in the evening was held up, so I invited my friend to be my guest at my parents' apartment. No one had told me that my mother was in hospital (she had had a minor eye operation), and I was surprised to find the apartment empty when I arrived. I didn't have any time to think: Giulietta was dying of thirst and I hurriedly put down the suitcases and opened the refrigerator. I found a bottle of 7-Up and gave it to Giulietta. Scarcely had she gulped down half the liquid when she had to throw up. She told me later that it had a strange taste: she thought it must have been kerosene. Worried and upset, I ran to the telephone and called my father at the pharmacy. He advised me to give Simionato some milk right away and to run to the hospital, when Simionato had calmed down, to ask my mother what infernal concoction she had put in the bottle. I went there and I can't forget with what disconcerting frankness my mother calmly answered, "It isn't kerosene, it's insecticide."

The hours that followed were among the most distressing of my life. Simionato continued to feel bad, and I had completely lost my head. At last I managed to track down my godfather, who, as I already had occasion to say, is the director of the Orthopedic Institute of New York, and I told him everything, asking him anxiously for advice. But instead of calming me down, his words increased my terror. I learned from him, in fact, that if a disaster occurred, I would be accused of having poisoned my Italian colleague, because when the incident took place there was no one at my house who could testify exactly how the events had unfolded. Just a few evenings ago, when we were seated together at the Biffi-Scala, I revealed to Giulietta the real nature of that "disinfectant." Until then I had never had the courage.

The season at Mexico City took place among many difficulties, also due to the terrible climate. I won't tell you about them, because if I lingered over every episode in my life I would fill two or three volumes. Here I have to make a digression. At that time I never felt well; I continually felt the effects of influenza, I suffered from nausea, and I had pains in my bones. But as always, I continued to sing. Upon my return from Mexico I granted myself three weeks of rest and immediately accepted Maestro Cuccia's proposal that I take part in Rossini's comic opera Il *Turco in Italia*, an offer that particularly cheered me (I, too, certainly have the right to amuse myself once in a while) because it allowed me to get away from the theme, by then habitual, of the grand tragedies in music, to breathe the fresh air of a very comical Neapolitan adventure. While I was preparing in Rome, under the direction of Maestro Gavezzani, I had the chance to become better acquainted with Luchino Visconti, who even before that had always paid me compliments, but whom I had never had the opportunity to get to know better. I remember my amazement at seeing a man of his distinction attentively observing almost all the rehearsals of

Turco, which lasted a minimun of three or four hours and were repeated twice a day. Beginning then Luchino Visconti endeared himself to me with his limitless admiration and precious friendship, and our close collaboration in the last few years was born precisely out of that mutual esteem.

I was saying that I never felt well. My husband didn't know what to attribute my condition to, but discovered it later when, unknown to me, he had a letter from my mother translated, as a consequence of which I was so upset that I had to take to my bed. He read it and found it full of recrimination, unjust accusation, and rash deduction. He couldn't control himself and replied to my mother on his own. He told her among other things that in order to marry me he had to go against his family, that my happiness was his life's aim, and that therefore he would not allow my mother to do anything that would distress me. Another painful exchange of letters followed, and we ended up, unfortunately, breaking off relations.

I beg the readers' pardon for this long digression, which has cost me great effort, and I take up my autobiography again. We are at the end of 1950. Among my engagements I had a *Parsifal* at the Rome RAI, *Don Carlo* at Naples and Rome, and then, on January 15, 1951, my first *Traviata* in Rome. I sang *Parsifal* and at the same time prepared for *Don Carlo* under the direction of Maestro Serafin. But during the rehearsals my health worsened to the point where I couldn't even swallow a sip of water. Battista then refused to listen to my arguments and forced me to return to Verona, where as soon as we arrived I took to my bed with a case of jaundice. I was immobilized by that irksome illness, and I had plenty of time to reflect on my family woes and to conclude that I must watch out, first of all, for my health and my husband's peace of mind.

I was replaced for the performance at Naples and Rome, but I didn't want to give up *Traviata* as well. For that reason, on Epiphany, barely able to get to my feet (for more than a month I had been fed solely milk), I went to Florence and began studying. As God willed it, the dress rehearsal arrived and I had a tiff with Maestro Serafin, who scolded me for turning up at the theater with too modest an air, dressed casually, and in general for not behaving, in his opinion, like a prima donna. I told him that I preferred to have people like me for my simplicity: colleagues (a vain illusion), chorus members, orchestra players, and everyone who lives around the stage (that's not an illusion). It was, however, a tiff without consequence, and the *Traviata* went very well. Immediately afterward I opened the Palermo season with *Norma*, and there I received a phone call from the director of La Scala, Antonio Ghiringhelli.

He asked me to come to see him as soon as I returned to Milan, which I did. But he had only a proposal: that I take over Tebaldi's *Aidas*, because Renata was indisposed. The preceding April, on the occasion of the Fair, I had been offered *Aida* at La Scala, and after much persuasion on the part of the management, I decided to accept. But after those performances, as has happened to me other times, I learned nothing more, and other opportunities to cross the threshold of the greatest opera theater in the world hadn't presented themselves. For that reason I told Ghiringhelli clearly and directly that I considered myself a singer worthy of having her own operas on the schedules and not just being used to take over operas already performed by others.

Then I went in Florence, for *Vespri Siciliani*; in the meantime Toscanini couldn't find a Lady Macbeth to suit him and had suggested my name for an audition. But when his daughter Wally asked a Milan theatrical agency for my address, she couldn't get it. She was told, moreover, that I was difficult, near hysteric or nearly, and that I would never agree to be auditioned by Toscanini. In any event, Wally didn't give up and tracked me down another way. Toscanini – I recall this episode with infinite emotion, the more so as the great Maestro is dead – heard me and offered me the part in *Macbeth*, which was to be produced at Bussetto. But just then, as readers will recall, the first alarm bells about Maestro's health were sounded, and he was obliged to give himself a little rest. And I lost the marvellous opportunity (which would later turn out to be the last, unfortunately) and the greatly coveted, extraordinary privilege of being directed by him.

While I was singing *Vespri Siciliani* in Florence I at last had a visit that was decisive for my career: that of Ghiringhelli, who this time had come to offer me the opening of the 1951-52 Scala seasons in *Vespri*. My contract additionally called for *Norma*, *The Abduction from the Seraglio*, and some performances of *Traviata* that didn't take place, for reasons that I don't know or don't wish to discuss, because by now it isn't worth the trouble. I accepted with joy, it goes without saying, and while waiting for that longed-for goal, I took part, although reluctantly, in a series of performances in Sao Paulo and Rio de Janeiro. In Sao Paulo I was supposed to open the season with *Aida* and afterward sing *Traviata*. Nevertheless, a few days before leaving, I received the news from Sao Paulo that, yes, I would open the season with *Aida*, but that the "prima" of *Traviata* had been assigned to Tebaldi, while the second performance had been reserved for me. I assure you – and I beg you to believe me – that I didn't fret about that. On the contrary, I consented willing to take over my colleague's *Traviata* twice.

I arrived in Sao Paulo with my legs swollen, as usual (I'll tell you later the reason for this persistent swelling), and in far from good health. For that reason, after the dress rehearsal of *Aida*, which went very well, I had to give up the prima, to my great desolation, and I was compensated for it only by the great success I had in *Norma* in Rio de Janeiro. It was in Rio that the first clashes between Renata and me occurred. We hadn't met for a long time and were very happy to see each other (at least I sincerely was). I remember that we were always together, in Rio's merry restaurant: I, she, her mother, Battista, and Elena Nicolai and her husband. Then, one fine day, Barretto Pinto, the director of the Opera Theatre (a rather odd man, but quite powerful in the financial and political fields, married to one of the wealthiest women in Brazil), invited the singers to take part in a benefit concert. I don't know – and still don't know – for whom or what that concert was organized; at any rate, we accepted, and Renata proposed – we were all in agreement with her – not to grant even a single encore. But when her turn came, she ended the "Ave Maria" from *Otello* halfway through because of the applause and, to our great surprise, launched into an aria from *Andrea Chenier* and immediately afterward "Vissi d'arte" from *Tosca*.

I was very taken aback (I had prepared only my usual bravura piece, "Sempre libera" from *Traviata*), but I attached to Renata's action the same weight that one would give to a child's caprice. Only later, during the supper that followed the concert, I realized that my dear colleague and friend had changed in her attitude toward me, that she couldn't manage to hide a certain tinge of bitterness every time she had to address me. Then I remembered that a short time before, when she entered the theater, she had passed in front of me without a gesture of greeting; and that at *Norma*, on meeting me in the corridor at the end of the performance, she had said to me in a somewhat spiteful tones: "Brava, Callas," calling me "Callas" for the first time, rather than "Maria." It was a matter of shadings, it's true, but I was upset by it. Later – we were eating at a round table and Nicolai was also with us – Renata began

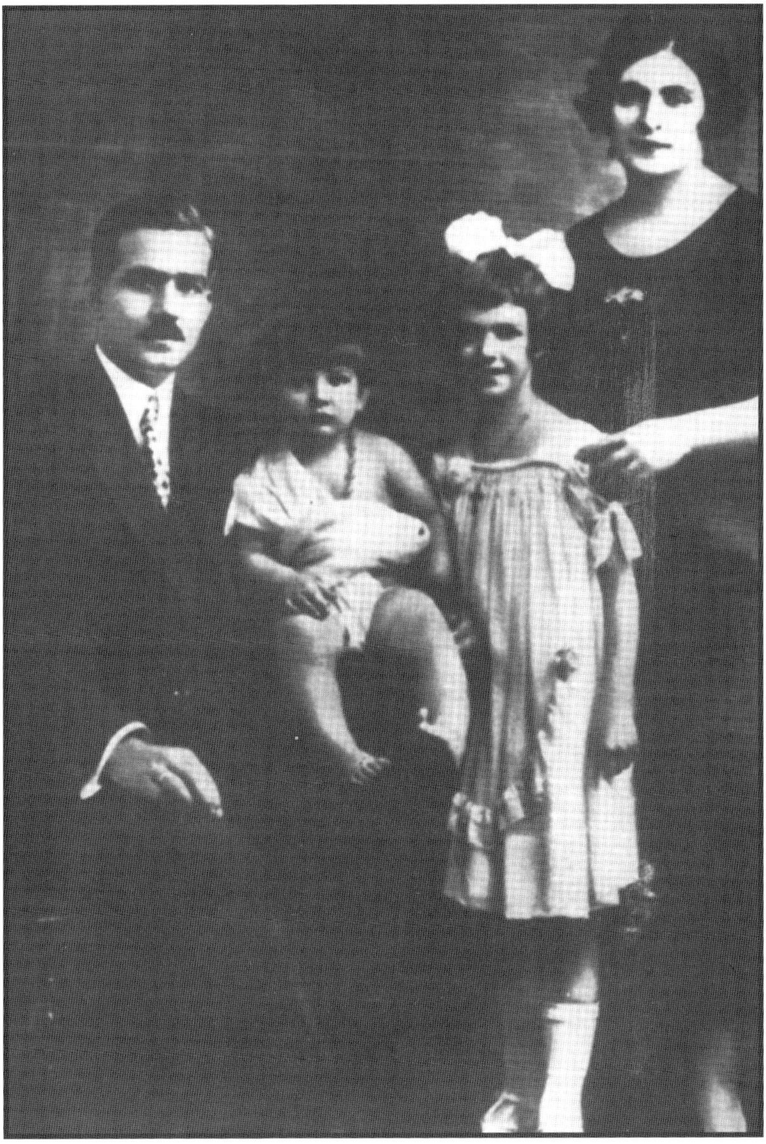

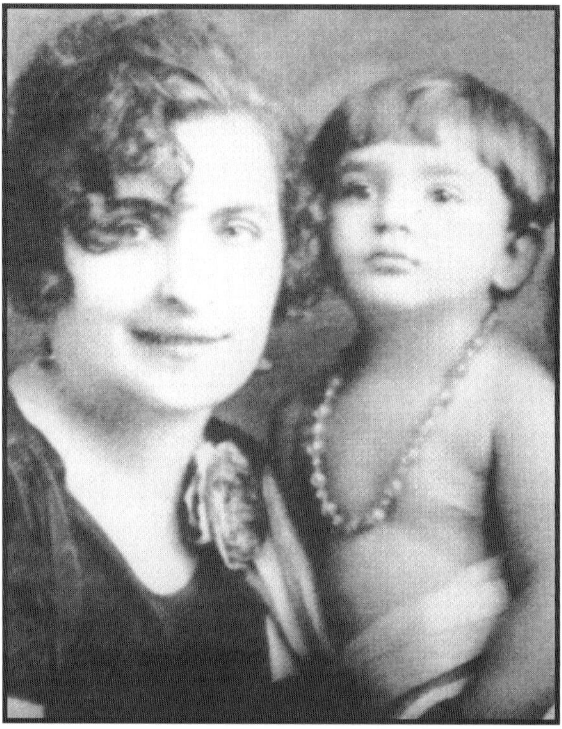

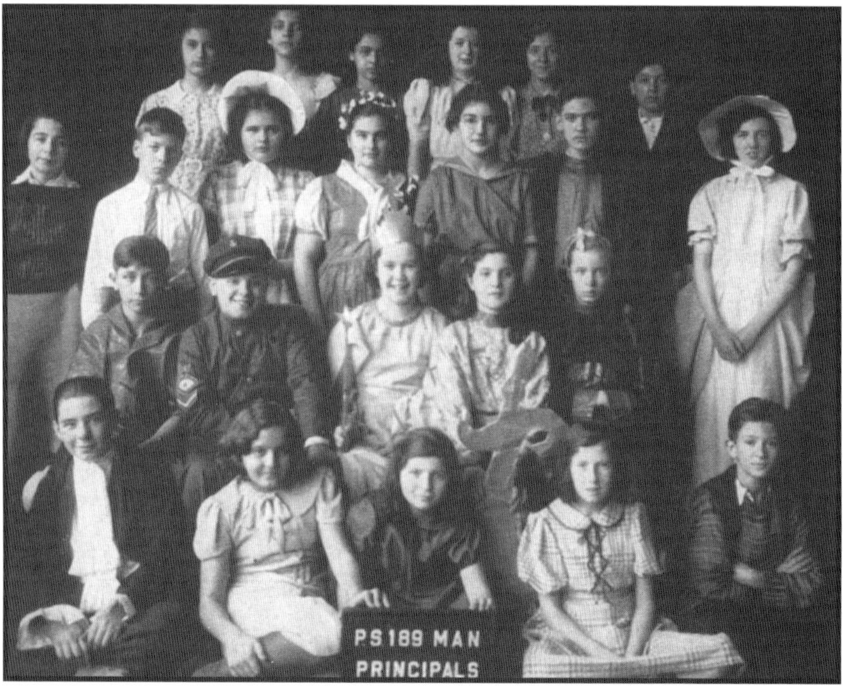
PS 189 MAN
PRINCIPALS

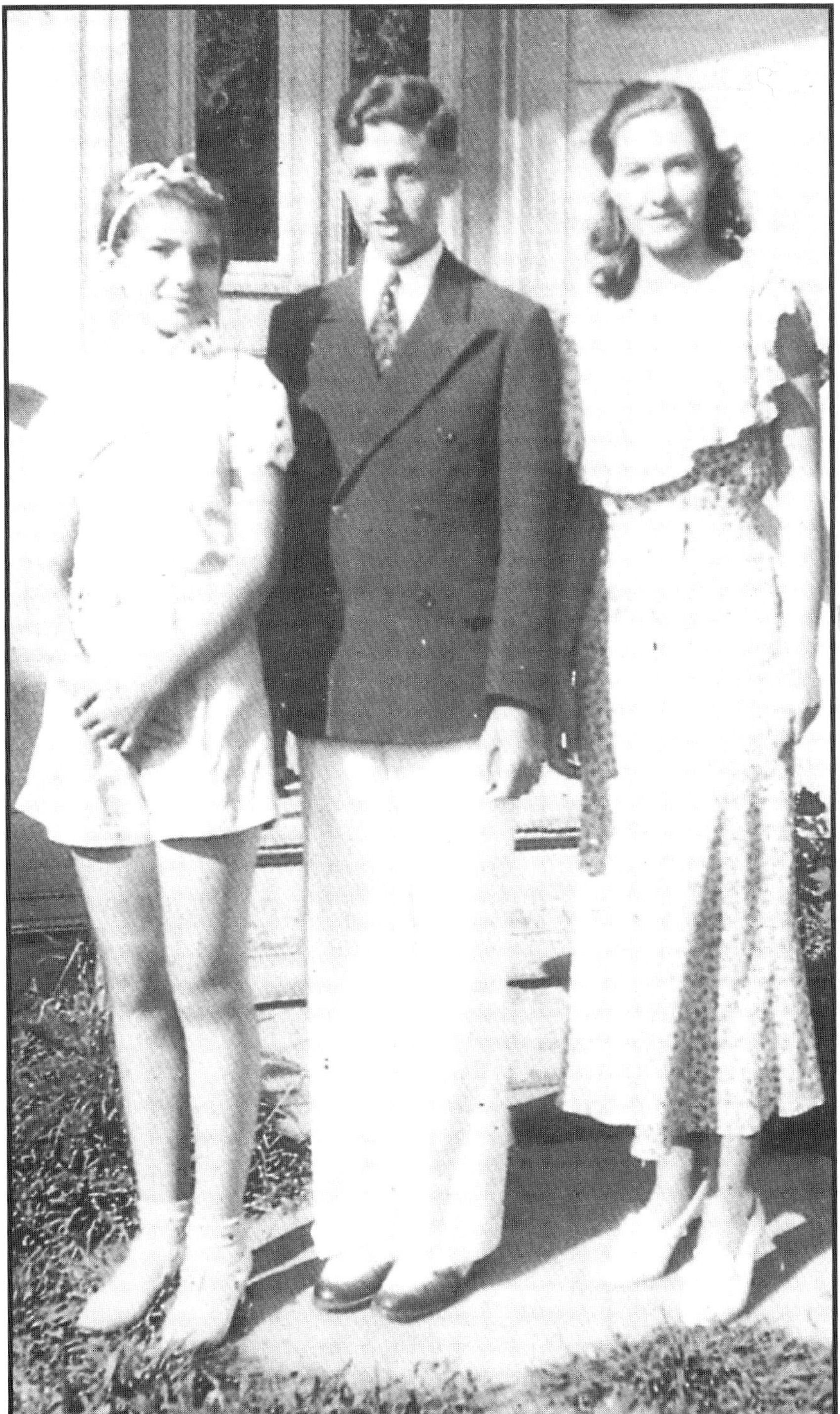

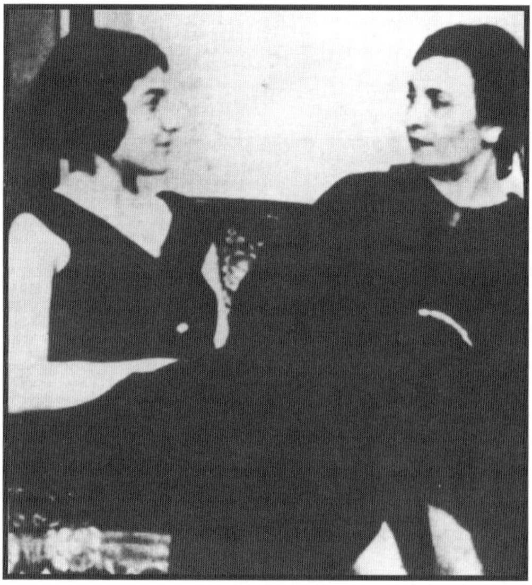

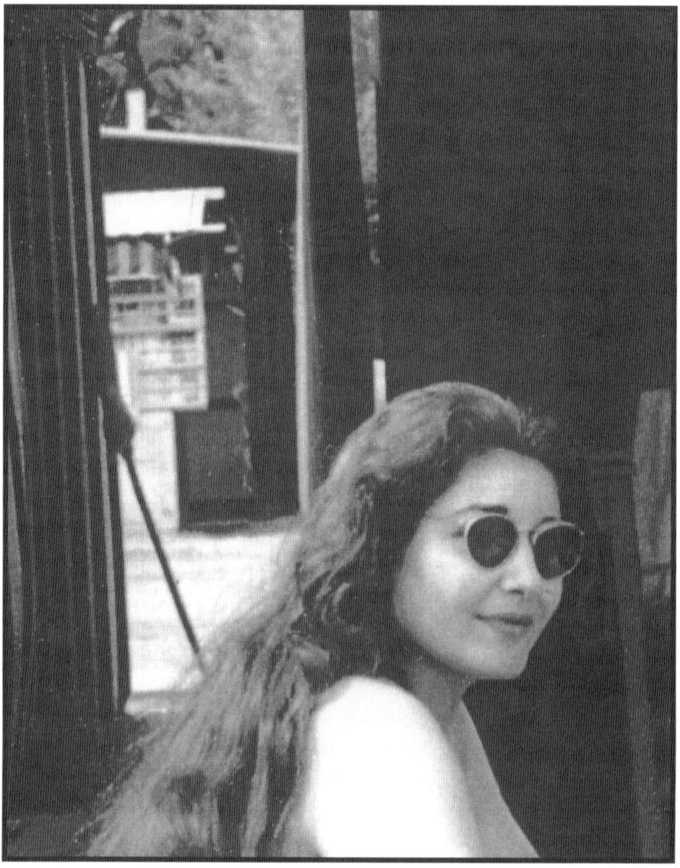

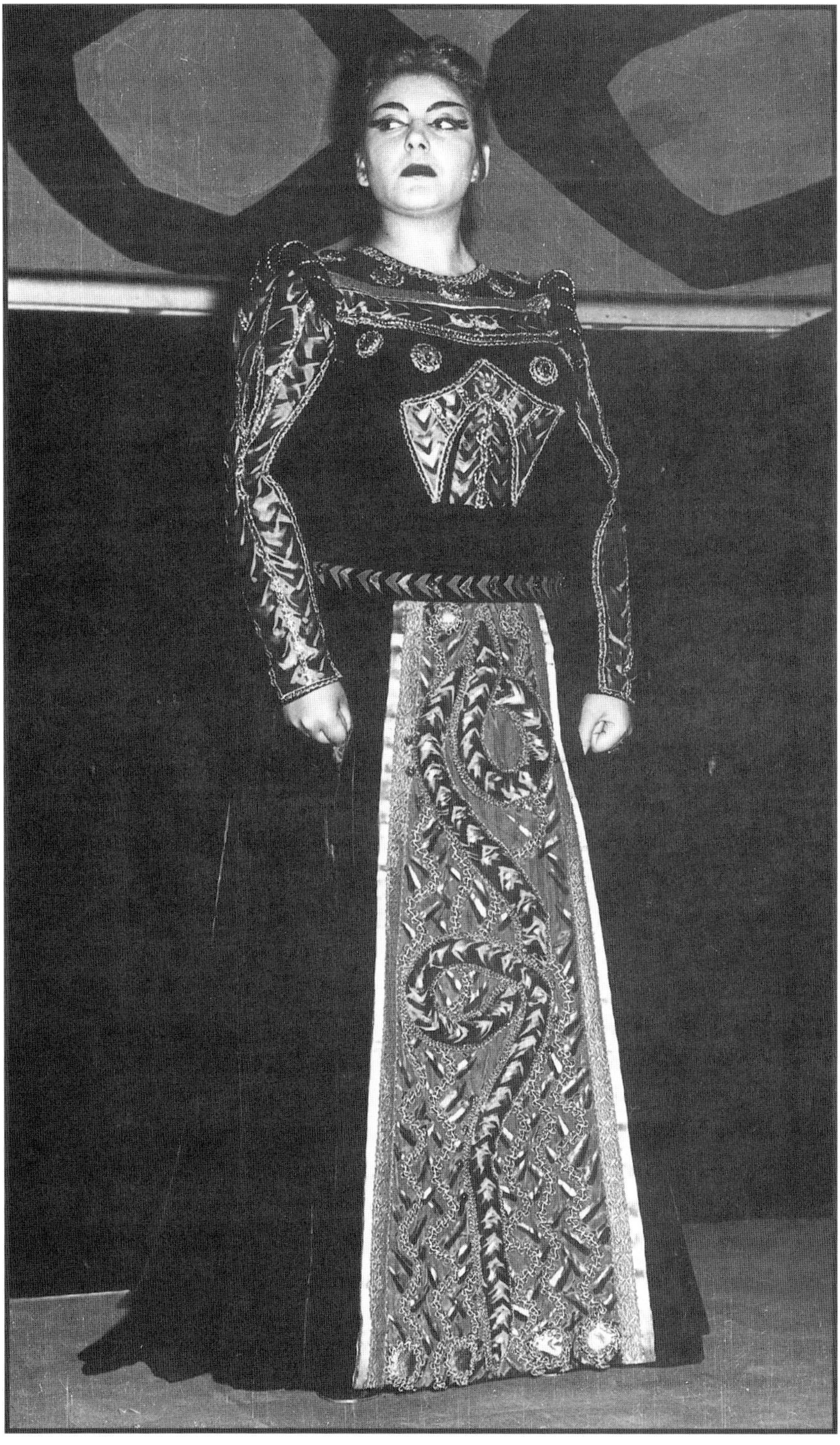

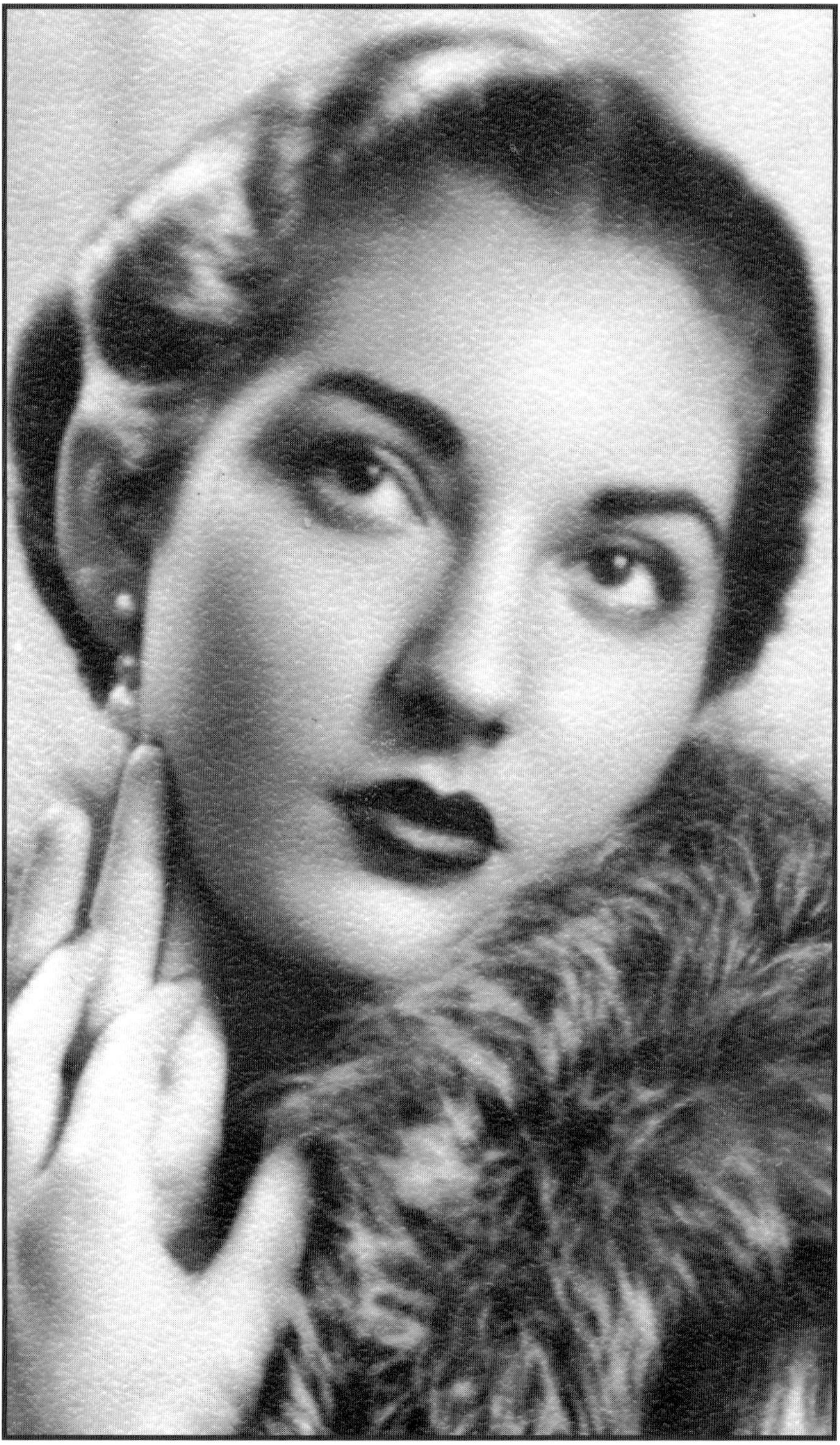

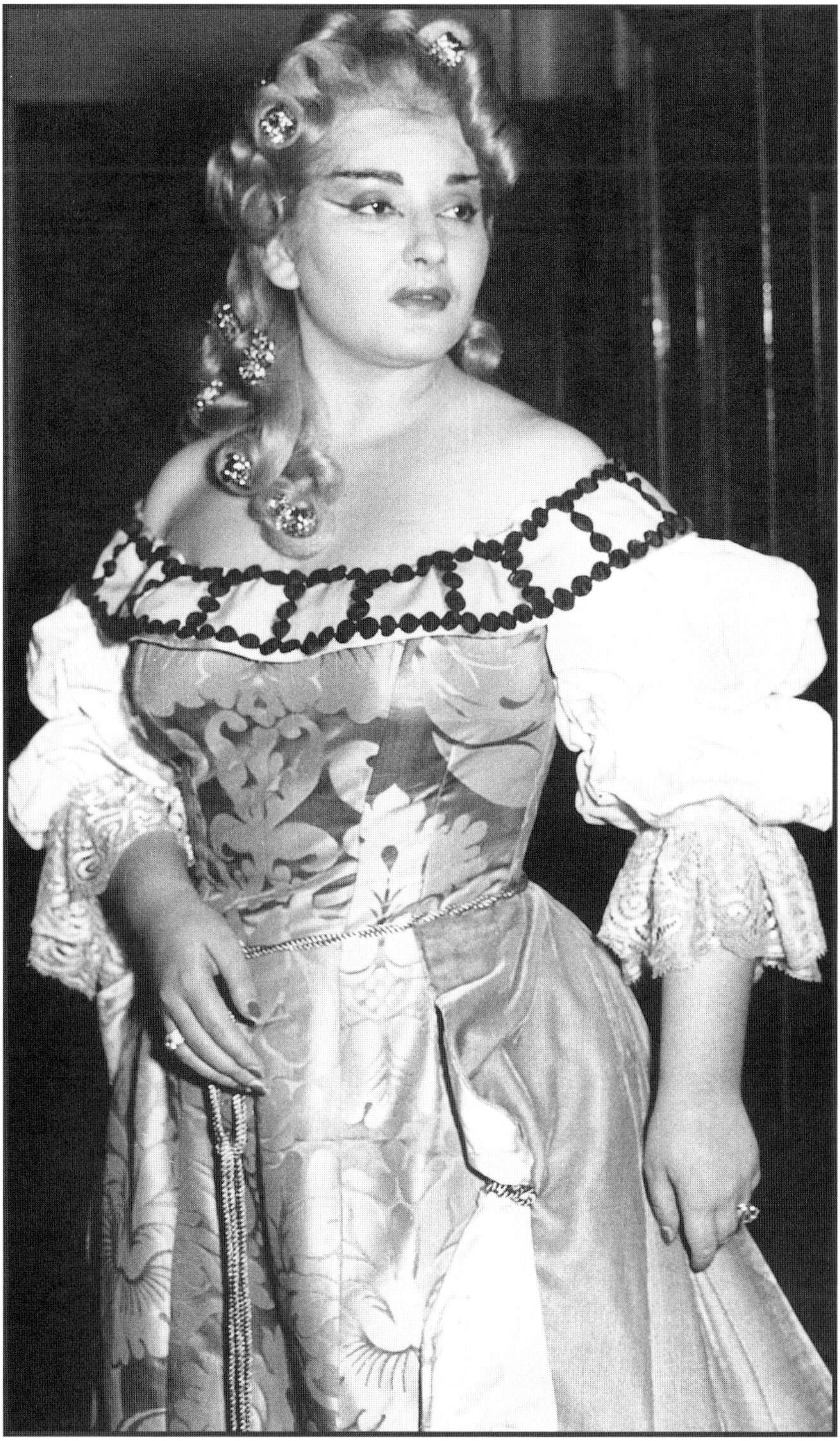

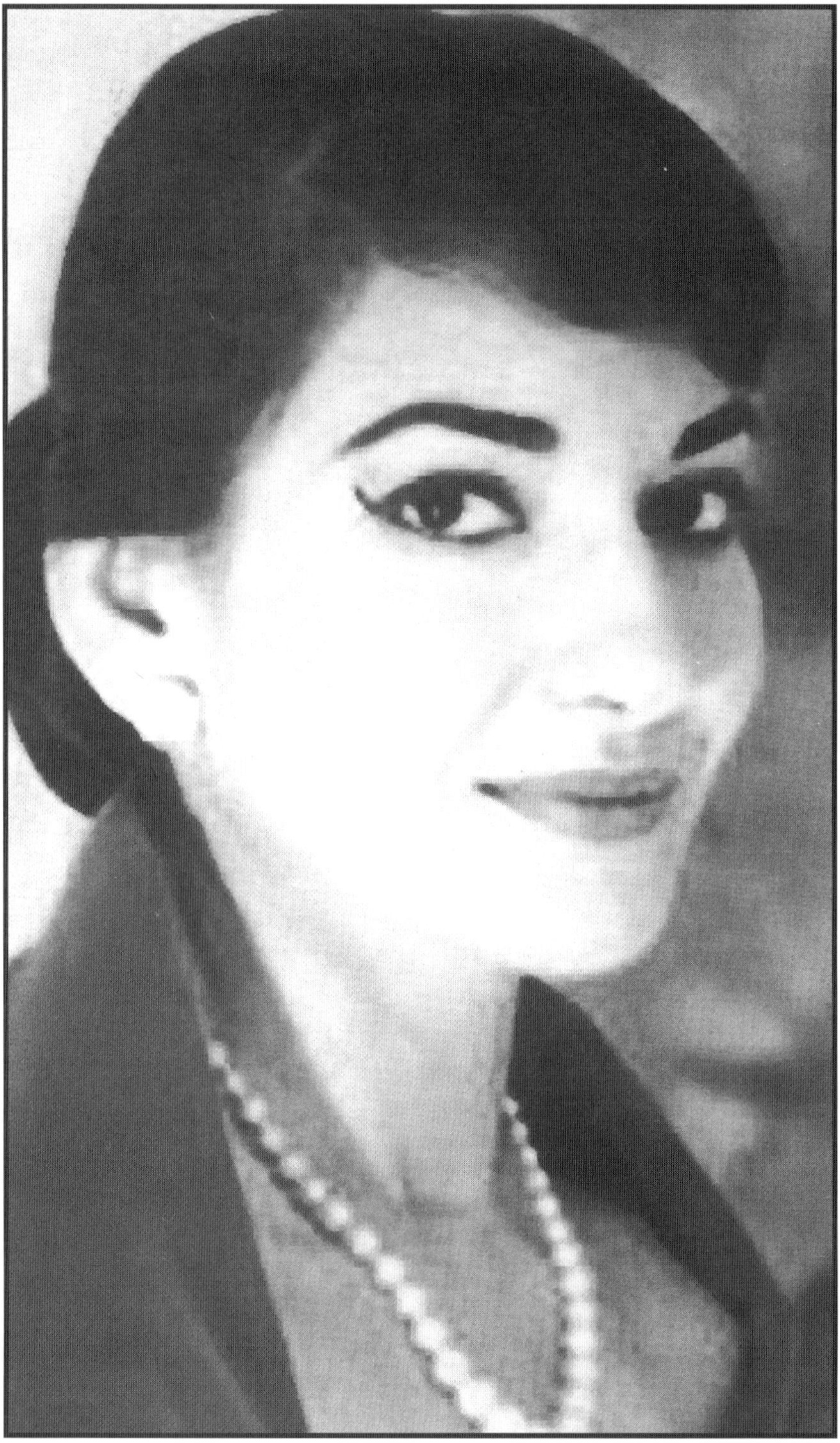

speaking of her alleged failure in *Traviata* at La Scala, warning me of the difficulties that I, too, would meet, as it seemed to her, in Milan. I replied rather brightly, and I remember that Titta nudged me with his elbow to get me to end the discussion. But everything would have been left there, with that exchange of views, a rather animated one, it has to be admitted, if the *Tosca* incident had not occurred.

5

After the benefit concert in Rio de Janeiro, Renata Tebaldi left for Sao Paulo, where she was to sing *Andrea Chenier*. I remained in Rio, waiting for the prima of *Tosca*. The discussion between Renata and me about La Scala had not left any traces: our relations had remained cordial, even if, perhaps, a bit less affectionate. But during my performance of *Tosca* a regrettable incident occurred. I had just finished the second act aria when I heard someone cry out amid the applause the name of another singer, Elisabetta Barbato, and I perceived a certain dissension in a part of the audience. I managed to control myself, not to allow myself to be defeated by humiliation and panic, and at the end of the performance I had the comfort of a long, warm ovation. Nevertheless, on the next day the director of the Opera Theatre, Barretto Pinto, of whom I've already had occasion to speak, summoned me to his office and without wasting words told me that I wouldn't be able to sing the subscription performances. In the other words, I had been "protested," as they say in theatrical parlance.

At first, because of the surprise, I couldn't manage to say even a single word; but then (I always rebel when I feel myself struck unjustly) I reacted very quickly. I yelled that my contract included, besides *Tosca* and *Gioconda* –

subscription performances only – two non-subscription performances of *Traviata*, and that he would have to pay me for them, even if he prevented me from singing them. Barretto Pinto flew into a rage. "All right," he told me (he had no other way out), "go ahead and sing *Traviata*, but I warn you right now that no one will come to hear you." He was a bad prophet, because the theater was sold out at both performances. Nevertheless, he couldn't resign himself to the burning defeat and tried to throw various obstacles my way. I remember very well that when I went to him to collect my pay, he spoke these precise words to me: "With the catastrophe that you had, I shouldn't even pay you." At that point I could no longer see straight and blindly grabbed the first object on his desk within reach, to throw at his head. And if someone hadn't been quick enough to seize me by the arm and restrain me, I don't know what would have happened.

I've revealed about this unpleasant episode in my career because it's linked to other bitter developments as well. As I've told you, while I was singing *Tosca* in Rio de Janeiro, Renata was singing *Andrea Chenier* in Sao Paolo. Naturally, since I'd been "protested" – and in that way – I was curious to learn the name of the soprano who had taken over in *Tosca*. And I had the sorrow of finding out that it was Renata, the singer whom I had always considered more a very dear friend than a colleague. It was said in addition that Tebaldi had ordered a copy of the costumes I had worn in *Tosca* from the dressmaker's shop that had made them for me; not just that, but it was added that she had gone to try them on herself, and all that before leaving for Sao Paolo, that is, when no one could know that I would be "protested."

Even now, every time that I look back on these now distant facts, I repeat to myself that Renata cannot have wanted to so disrupt our good friendship, and that perhaps there is a painful and incomprehensible misunderstanding at the bottom of all of this. And even if the circumstances seemed unfavourable to her and those around her, I try to persuade myself that this is surely just a misunderstanding between us, and I continue to hope sincerely that it can be resolved someday.

After the unhappy interval in Rio, I returned to Italy. I was disappointed and hurt, but I needed all my energy and all my enthusiasm: I was to open the La Scala season for the first time, and I thought I had never faced such a difficult test in all my life. But the welcome that the Milan public gave my *Vespri Siciliani*, under Maestro de Sabata's direction, was enough to remove doubts, and in the subsequent performances I was already sure of myself, proud of having conquered the most demanding audience in the world.

Afterwards I gave Rossini's *Armida* in Florence (I had to learn it in five days), closed the Rome season with *Puritani*, and then left for Mexico, where among other things I sang *Lucia,* a rather challenging opera that I wanted to try out abroad before including it in my repertory in Italy.

On returning from Mexico I sang *Gioconda* and *Traviata* at the Verona Arena and then, in September or October, went to London for several performances of *Norma*. It was my debut in England, and I remember that the moment I stepped onto the stage, I thought that my heart had suddenly stopped beating. I had been preceded in London by sensational publicity, and I was terrified by the idea of being unable to live up to expectations. It's always like that, for us artists: we labour for years to make ourselves known, and when fame finally follows our steps everywhere, we are condemned always to be worthy of it, to outdo ourselves so as not to disappoint the public, which expects wonders of its idols. And we, unfortunately, are only human, with the frailness of our nature. I, for instance, am considered a very sensitive actress; but that sensitivity complicates my already arduous work incredibly. When I sing, even if I seem calm, I suffer the unbearable fear of not being able to give my best. Our voice is a mysterious instrument that often deals us sad surprises, and there's nothing we can do but turn to the Lord at the beginning of a performance and say to Him with humility, "We are in Thy hands."

I'm not superstitious, or perhaps I am, but in a way different from others: but I can never part with a little portrait in oil, attributed to Cignaroli, of the Madonnina. That little canvas, which was given to me by my husband on the occasion of my first *Gioconda* at Verona, accompanies me everywhere; I whine if I don't have it in my dressing room. Perhaps it's pure coincidence; however, twice I forgot to take it with me and in both cases I was obliged, not because of any fault of mine, to give up the performances. For that reason, last year, when I realized I'd forgotten the precious little portrait (I was in Vienna for Lucia), I hurried to call one of my friends in Milan and begged her to come to Austria immediately to deliver the Madonnina to me.

Let's return to the "prima" of *Norma* at Covent Garden in London. In spite of my apprehensions, the performance went very well and I had a warm reception from the audience. I returned to Milan to open the 1952-53 Scala season with Verdi's *Macbeth*. But during the performance, immediately after the sleepwalking scene, I distinctly heard two or three whistles amid the applause. It wasn't the usual whistling done with the lips: it was quite obvious that the disrupter was using a real whistle. I felt rather bad, and the wonderful public, so impartial and generous, took up my defence, turning my success into a triumph. Nevertheless, the whistler didn't become discouraged and made his presence known to me at the performances of *Gioconda* and *Trovatore*. Since then he's never been missing when I sing at La Scala. By now I'm used to it: I'll say even more, I've almost become fond of it.

After finishing the *Trovatore* performances and a concert tour of various Italian cities, I sang Cherubini's *Medea* in Florence. As usual, I had had to study the score in eight days, and this time it was a challenging part with regard to interpretation, too: the enthusiasm that I provoked – it was a truly unforgettable performance – stupefied me and elated me.

In June I set out for London again, where the official ceremonies for the coronation of Elizabeth II were underway. I sang *Aida*, *Norma*, and *Trovatore*. Then I returned to Italy, and between the performances of *Aida* at the Verona Arena and those of *Norma* at Trieste, I could allow myself a bit of rest. But during the performances of *Norma* I had to shuttle frequently between Milan and Trieste: the new Scala season was approaching and the management, at a certain moment, had decided to replace *Mitridate* (which was supposed to be performed between *La Wally*, the season opener, and *Rigoletto*) with Cherubini's *Medea*. The opera was to be directed by Maestro Bernstein, but to my amazement, he showed himself reluctant to accept the assignment. I learned at last – and my amazement was diminished – that he had been advised by a group of "friends" who, to frighten him, had spoken to him at length of my difficult personality, my scenes, and so on. In any event, the management of La Scala made an appointment for me with Bernstein; and as soon as he heard me, he put any uncertainties aside.

At that time the newspapers were beginning to talk, in as veiled a way as possible, of an alleged rivalry between Tebaldi and me, and I remember that precisely on the occasion of *La Wally* I read in the columns of *L'Europeo* sage advice from a dear friend, the writer and music critic Emilio Radius. Why, said Radius, don't these two singers publicly shake hands in order to silence the gossip and eloquently demonstrate that there is no rancour between them? Since Rio de Janeiro I hadn't had further occasion to meet Renata, and Radius's words gave me the idea of going to hear *La Wally*, which was sung by her, and to salute her from a box. I thought to pay homage to her in that way and was convinced that the next day, at my *Medea*, Tebaldi would reciprocate. So I went to La Scala to applaud my fine colleague with warmth, as she certainly deserved; I smiled at her often, to make my intentions understood, and I expected a sign or a salute from her that would have authorized me to visit her in her dressing room. But that sign and that signal weren't forthcoming, and Renata wasn't at the "prima" of *Medea*. She was present, however, at the third (or fourth) performance of the opera, because my husband saw her enter the box where he was, just at the moment the curtain rose. Battista greeted her cordially, helped her remove her fur, and asked after her mother. There was a polite reply, but even today Titta is convinced that he wasn't recognized, In fact, as he told me, soon after my entrance Tebaldi rose to her feet, nervous and irritated, and hastily putting on her fur, left the box without saying good-bye, and slamming the door.

That season at La Scala marked two of my greatest successes: the first in *Medea* and the second in *Lucia*. Apropos of *Lucia* I remember that after the sextet I made the tenor Giuseppe Di Stefano go out by himself to receive the audience's applause. (He was still depressed by a not very happy performance of *Rigoletto* and needed some injections of enthusiasm.) I'm recalling that not to give myself any special credit, but because, as you know, I am constantly accused of never allowing my colleagues to share with me the joy of an ovation.

In October, after singing *Mefistofele* at Verona, I left for Chicago, where I was engaged for *Norma*, *Traviata*, and *Lucia*, and on my return I opened the 1954-55 Scala season with *La Vestale*, entrusting myself for the first time to Luchino Visconti's direction. Right after *Vestale* the schedule called for *Trovatore*, but the tenor, Mario del Monaco, suddenly refused to take part in the performance because, he said, he had had an attack of appendicitis. *Trovatore* was then replaced with *Andrea Chenier*, and so I had to learn that opera in five days. In return, naturally, I was accused of having provoked the substitution myself. We went on with *Andrea Chenier*, and at the third-act aria the usual monotonous nuisances made themselves heard, as always. At the end of the performances of *Andrea Chenier*, I myself proposed that Mario del Monaco, who was to leave for America, take a solo bow: first of all because he was the protagonist of the opera, and then because it was the last performance at La Scala of the year. Mario del Monaco has never spoken of that gesture of mine. Instead, an incredible story about my "kick in the shins" has been spread. As you know, according to that fantastic account, during the performance of *Norma* I allegedly gave him such a violent kick in the shins that it made him groan and limp, in order to prevent him from taking a curtain call with me!

It's better for me to continue my autobiography, which is now approaching the last chapter. We're at the end of 1955 and are preparing for the "prima" of *Traviata*. The rehearsals went on in an exhausting way, because of the listless collaboration of certain colleagues, especially the tenor, Di Stefano, who was never punctual. In the evening, then, we waited for him for hours, because Di Stefano – as he affirmed candidly – couldn't sing before midnight.

Mortally tired, we arrived at the "prima," and after going out in front of the curtain all together many, many times, I took a solo bow, at the invitation of Maestro Guilini and of Luchino Visconti. At that point Di Stefano left, slamming his dressing room door. The following day he went to his Ravenna villa, and we, on the eve of the "seconda," were without a tenor. Fortunately, Giacinta Prandelli kindly agreed to take over the opera and we were able (no one is indispensable) to continue the performance.

I forgot to say that as *Traviata* approached, several anonymous letters (I received them, too; it is not, unfortunately, a privilege just of Tebaldi's) had forewarned me that I would be whistled. Instead, to my great surprise, no one caused any disruptions either at the "prima" or the "seconda," and I was particularly happy about that unexpected truce. But it was only a trick to make the snare more dangerous. In fact, when, at the third performance, right after the attack on "Gioir," I heard a kind of roar from the gallery, and – out of surprise – I was about to cut the note short, and my rebellion was such that it was felt, I think, even by the audience. That evening (there were also many critics in the theater who had been notified by anonymous letters and calls to come to hear me because "there would be a chance to have some fun") it was I – I declare it openly – who demanded that none of my colleagues go out before the curtain with me. I wanted the audience to tell me its opinion clearly and straightforwardly, and the audience did so, with a generous rain of applause that extinguished my fury.

In September, after a period of rest, alternated with intense preparations for recordings, I sang two performances of *Lucia* in Berlin, heading then to Chicago, for the second time, to open the season: I had in my program *Puritani*, *Trovatore*, and *Butterly*, which was repeated a third time, as an exception. My season at Chicago was concluding. But while I was waving to the audience, bowing to the applause, in the wings someone was transacting – I don't have words to describe my disgust – my "delivery" to the process servers; that is, to those who presented the summons.

Many of my readers will remember having seen in the newspapers the photograph of an incensed and enraged Callas who was threatening and demanding justice. I was not indignant at the poor process servers, who in the final analysis were carrying out orders they had received (in America a citation is not valid if the person who delivers it doesn't meet the addressee), but at those who had kept silence about the trap and ignobly betrayed me.

I returned to Italy and opened the Scala season for the fourth time, with *Norma*, and on that occasion had the usual accompaniment of nuisances and the usual discussions with my colleagues. One of them, a woman, more animated than the others, threw herself between my husband and Mario del Monaco, who didn't know to whom to pour out his blazing irritation for a summons that had arrived for him that very day.

In January 1956 La Scala revived *Traviata*, and at this point I should talk about "the drama of the turnips," but it's an old story by now. It's true, at the end of the performance I gathered up a bunch of turnips, mistaking them for flowers because of my nearsightedness. Some carrots fell from the gallery, rolling between the hands of Luchino Visconti, who was in the prompter's box and was dying of laughter. They were vegetables that were out of season, which for that reason couldn't have been purchased at a regular stall before the performance, but revealed a prearranged plan, careful preparation. Indeed, who goes to the theater with turnips in his pocket? However, those pitiful gestures always turn to the disadvantage of the person who performs them, or rather, the person who suggests them: and I have long since ceased to be grieved by that business. After "the drama of the turnips" I sang *Lucia* in Naples; I was again at La Scala, in *Il Barbiere* and in *Fedora*, and then at Vienna in *Lucia*. At Vienna a certain colleague arranged the usual yelling against me. At the end of the opera I had only one wish: to get out of my costume, remove my makeup, and leave the theater. But Maestro von Karajan begged me to go before the curtain with him, because it is a custom in Vienna that the conductor take a solo curtain call at the end of the performance: and there was someone who disliked that. But in any event, one gets used to everything, and my colleagues' caprices no longer upset me.

But now I say this with infinite tiredness, I had to begin again from the beginning, because the tangle of caprices, resentments, grudges, and rumors has become public property, to the point of impelling me to this open, frank, and painful confession. Last November, as you know, I went to New York to sing at the Metropolitan. I had heard Mr. Bing spoken of a great deal, and from what had been related to me, I was a little prejudiced against him. Instead I found in him a perfect gentleman, an exquisite and solicitous director. While I was preparing *Norma*, an article about me appeared in *Time* magazine that repeated a number of commonplaces that were for the most part figments of the imagination. I wanted to refute those reports, but I thought that time, as always, would be the best avenger. Instead, that article had the power to influence the American public unfavourably in its attitude toward me; it was picked up immediately by the Italian press and has become a weapon, in the hands of my enemies, for an absurd and unjust campaign against me.

Unfortunately, I am now obliged to defend myself, to excuse myself from blows that I never dealt. It is not true that at the Metropolitan the turnips "encore" occurred: if I had received vegetables in homage in America, too, I would calmly tell you about it, as I did with regard to *Traviata*. It is not true that when interviewed by the *Time* correspondent, I told him: "Renata Tebaldi is not like Callas; she lacks backbone." That phrase, besides, was attributed – and for anyone who can read English there can be no doubt about it – not to me, but to a third party. Moreover, I don't understand why Renata is offended by those innocuous words. What should I say, then, about an article that treated topics that ought not even to be touched on, such as those concerning the relations between my mother and me?

Of the accusation, publicly tossed at me by Renata, of "lacking a heart"? I am only cheered that my colleague, in her letter to the editor of *Time*, finally decided to confess that she herself wanted to keep her distance from La Scala, whose atmosphere, she explained, is "stifling" for her. That sincerely cheers me, because until recently, among the other innumerable accusations, I was also assailed with this one: of having impeded, with my diabolical arts, Renata Tebaldi's return to the stage of the theater that always loved her.

My story is finished. I have been sincere, perhaps even too much so. But there is only one truth, and it does not fear refutations. In a few days I'll sing at La Scala again, first in *Sonnambula*, then – for the Fair – in *Anna Bolena*, and finally, in *Iphigenie*. I know that my enemies are lying in wait for me; but I will fight, as much as is humanly possible, not to disappoint my public, which loves me and whose esteem and admiration I don't want to lose. "Watch out, Maria," my good friend, the celebrated critic Eugenio Gara, has often told me, "remember the Chinese proverb that says: 'He who rides the tiger can never dismount.'" No, dear Eugenio, don't be afraid: I'll do everything I can so as not to dismount my tiger.

REMEMBERING CALLAS

Some Confessions of a Fan

WILLIAM WEAVER

Southern climes can have a special kind of winter: not biting, but penetrating, subtly demoralizing, relentlessly damp. Among my worst winter memories is a cold snap in New Orleans that struck me like a paralysis. And, almost as bad, a chill, heavy December on the island of Ischia in 1949. Wystan Auden was in America, teaching somewhere; and for a month I shared his house with his life-long companion, my friend Chester Kallman. Needless to say, the house had no heating system; and when the cold was at its worst, I would gulp down a cup of morning coffee, go straight back to bed, huddle under all available blankets, and read until lunch time. Chester seldom got up before noon anyway, so for him the cold problem was already half-solved.

It was on one of those mornings, as we stumbled around the kitchen, probably hung over, scratching together some lunch, that I first heard the name of Maria Callas. Chester, as usual, had taken possession of the Naples newspaper. On the entertainment page he made a discovery that abruptly brought both of us to complete, keen wakefulness. The Teatro San Carlo announced a new production of Verdi's *Nabucco*. Now, in those days, even in Italy, the opera repertory was fairly limited, and of Verdi's twenty-odd works, perhaps only a half-dozen, the most popular, were given with any regularity.

For us *Nabucco* represented an incredible rarity, and – Verdians to the core – we immediately took steps to get tickets, reserve hotel rooms, decide which of the uncomfortable boats we would take to the mainland. As an afterthought I asked Chester who would be singing, and he read from the paper: the famous baritone Gino Bechi would interpret the title role; the soprano was Maria Callas.

I've heard the name, he added (Chester followed opera the way Hoosiers follow basketball), she's sung in Verona and in Venice; she's supposed to be good.

A few nights later we were in Naples, still in a state of overexcitement. All we knew of *Nabucco*'s music was the famous chorus "Va pensiero." We had been unable to procure a score or a libretto, so we got to the theater early to buy programs and learn the outline of the plot (an outline of the plot of *Nabucco* would look like the CAT scan of a severe schizophrenic).

Though wartime dust still coated the nineteenth-century statues and the marble balustrades, though paint peeled from walls and damp made crumbling scabs, the San Carlo was – as it still is – the most beautiful opera house in the world, the perfect setting for a memorable evening. The great chandelier went dark; for a few moments the dimmed light from the red-plush boxes made the house seem afire. Then only the pit glowed, and the conductor raised his baton. The prelude to *Nabucco* begins slowly, deceptively; but after a few bars there is a crashing chord and a scurrying allegro section that has all the energy and impatience of Verdi's early music: the music of a man who has a story to tell and wants to get on with it.

And it was. Orchestra and chorus outdid themselves in generous vigor ("Va pensiero," as always in Italy, had to be encored); but our attention was focused on Callas, in the role of the wicked, treacherous, finally penitent Abigaille, a complex, unlikable, and yet moving character. What I remember most vividly of Callas' interpretation that evening was the end of her great scene, "Ben io t'invenni," in which, having stolen a vital document, she is free to usurp the throne and expresses her determination to do that very thing.

The set was a challenge: a huge, steep flight of steps, with the throne on a confined platform at the top. Callas began the aria below the steps, then as she continued singing, she moved up the high flight, occasionally descending a step or two, as if physically to express her lingering hesitation about her plan; but then, as the aria ended, she climbed straight to the little platform and, on the final, ringing high note, she sat down squarely on the throne. Sitting down is not the usual way a soprano concludes a great scene. More likely, she will stride towards the footlights, or raise a triumphant arm, or – in more pathetic cases – faint. But Callas' taking her seat was such an unusual and dramatic assertion of power that the audience gave her an ovation.

During the aria – indeed, during the whole performance – I had admired Callas' apparent self-assurance. Unlike most of her colleagues, she sang the whole difficult and (in the way of Italian theaters then and now) probably under- rehearsed role without ever looking at the conductor. And yet she was always perfectly in time, every attack was clean, precise. Similarly, when she had to negotiate that menacing flight of stairs, she never once looked at her shoes or raised her skirts timidly, to avoid a tumble. She displayed total confidence.

Later I learned – as all her fans did – the simple reason why she never looked at the conductor: she couldn't see him. Tremendously near-sighted, during rehearsals she wore big, thick glasses and learned every position, every movement as thoroughly as she learned her notes. Then, once the performance was in progress, she moved entirely on instinct. This was an example of how she was able to turn a defect into a positive merit. Similarly, for the better part of her career she used the flaws in her voice, its tendency to turn harsh at times, in order to enhance the drama of the role, to add a dimension to the character. In her recording of *Butterfly* when she tells the intrusive marriage broker to leave, her "va via" chills the blood, in its shrill authority. Similarly, a few years later, in playing Anne Boleyn (Donizetti's *Anna Bolena*), when informed that she was to face a trial, she made the brief line, "Giudici! Ad Anna!" (Judges! For Anne!), unforgettable.

Chester and I left the theater with our heads in a whirl. Nowadays, when even Verdi's least known works are often performed and all have been recorded, it is hard to recapture the excitement of hearing one of those operas for the first time: like opening a drawer and discovering a great pile of dazzling jewels, like stumbling by accident into the Sistine Chapel. And the discovery of a new and great singer was another cause for sleeplessness. For an hour or more we wandered the dark, deserted streets of Naples, trying to remember some of the just-heard tunes, trying to find words to describe the strange, hauntingly individual voice whose acquaintance we had just made.

A short time after the New Year I went back to Rome where, in theory, I was a graduate student at the university. But I spent most of my time reading, trying to write a novel, and – on every occasion – opera-going. Callas actually had sung at the Rome Opera (as Kundry in *Parsifal* the previous year) but I had been briefly in America and the appearance had escaped me. Now she was to return, again in a Wagner role: Isolde, sung in an Italian translation, conducted by Tullio Serafin, the great, veteran maestro who had been her mentor in Italy since her early Venice performances.

That *Tristano e Isotta* was memorable, but not entirely for the right reasons. Some time before the premiere the Italian tenor scheduled to sing Tristan had defected, and the best solution the Rome Opera could find was to call in a German tenor – an artist, it proved, of no particular distinction – who was unable, of course, to learn the role in Italian, so he sang it in the original.

Callas, in a long red wig, was a demoniacal Isolde; her dress had a cape whose tips were attached to her little fingers so that, when she held her arms out, she resembled Batwoman. And her Brangaene, Elena Nicolai, similarly costumed, was equally hyperactive. The whole sense of the first act was transformed. This seemed to be the story of a poor man who, by mistake, had boarded the wrong ship, and unable to overcome the language barrier, kept getting himself in trouble with the two hysterical women in charge.

In those days, I should explain, I was not much of a Wagnerian and this was, in fact, my first exposure to *Tristan*. Soon I gave up trying to follow the drama, and allowed myself simply to enjoy the fluent, seductive direction of Serafin and the intensity of Callas' singing (there is a Callas recording of the "Liebestod" in Italian, and I listen to it often, partly because it is beautiful and partly because it carries me back to the Rome Opera of those days of revelations).

After the *Tristan* she made what I think of as her real debut at the Rome Opera, in *Norma* with Ebe Stignani as Adalgisa and Serafin again conducting. There were five performances, and I think I managed to get to four of them. Luchino Visconti – opera-lover as well as brilliant director – was always there, too, sitting with a group of friends squarely in the center of the front row, his favorite vantage point. At that time, a Callas performance did not automatically fill the theater, so tickets were fairly easy to come by. As I went to successive performances, I began to recognize faces in the house: the Callas audience was beginning, spontaneously, to form. Later, I would see those same faces in Milan, in London.

In that *Norma*, Callas had little help from the threadbare production. Nothing went terribly wrong with the staging, but nothing was exactly right, either. The chorus, for example, seemed to take forever to straggle off the stage, so when one character sang about the sacred wood being deserted, there were still a few sopranos pushing one another into the wings. Yet, those performances were for me the definitive confirmation of Callas' genius. At that time, her voice almost always obeyed her; she could soften it into a molten tenderness, with the faintest hint of – not a sob, but a little catch, a throb of irretrievable sadness; she could make it ring with a tone of command. For her famous first act prayer, "Casta Diva," she summoned a reverent, dream-like tone, but then, in the second part of the aria, as her thoughts turned from the chaste goddess to her truant lover, she introduced a pleading, somehow seductive strain, another tessera in the mosaic of her complex characterization. In a video tape of a Paris recital, without benefit of costume or set, she sings "Casta Diva" with the intensity and variety I recall from those Rome performances: the slightest movement of her head tells you the meaning of a word, a twitch of her stole, a flash of her eyes.

After her fame had become worldwide, writers narrating her early years often describe her as fat. And sometimes they even use the word clumsy. These adjectives are totally misleading. Clumsy, she never was; nor was she really fat, if that is taken to mean obese or grotesque. True, she was a big woman, Junoesque, heavy; but she knew – even then – how to move. Or rather how not to move. A single imperious gesture, her arm extended laterally, the forefinger firmly pointed, did more to establish Norma's drama than broad pacings or semaphore arm- waving. At that time, the much-publicized but genuine rivalry with Tebaldi was at its height. Tebaldi had the advantage, then, of physical beauty, a sweet and appealing face, and an irresistibly lovely voice; but, partly because of a slight physical defect, she moved awkwardly and, to compensate for her deficiencies as an actress, she had a tendency to flutter.

Callas also had an extra weapon: those eyes! They, too, were Junoesque, ox-like in their breadth and their liquid softness. Even when she was standing stock-still, her eyes would do her acting for her: warm for one instant, icy with scorn the next. In moments of indignation, they would blaze like coals. In *Norma*, where the libretto portrayed her in many contrasting situations, the eyes often told the story: she was priestess, lover, mother, daughter, judge, and victim. At the end of the last performance, like many in the audience, I had become not just a fan, but a worshipper; and after the last curtain call, I left bereft.

The season at the Rome Opera, in those days, was relatively short (from late December until spring); but there were smaller, more-or-less makeshift seasons in other theaters to fill the gaps in the opera-lover's calendar. So, in the autumn of 1950, several months after the *Norma*s and long before the opening of the official season, the Teatro Eliseo – usually devoted to spoken theater – was taken over by a group of Roman intellectuals and music-lovers who put together a little festival, which included modern works (a one-act opera by Goffredo Petrassi and a reconstruction of Cocteau's *Les Mariés de la Tour Eiffel*) as well as a Rossini rarity, *Il turco in Italia*. The director of the Rossini was an acquaintance of mine, Gerardo Guerrieri, and the prima donna was Maria Callas, supported by a cast of largely young singers, specialists in bel canto (the tenor was Cesare Valletti), plus the great Mariano Stabile, who had sung *Falstaff* with Toscanini in the twenties. The moment the announcement was made, I was electrified with anticipation and I asked Guerrieri – as a special favor – if I could attend some of the rehearsals.

The first one I was allowed to follow was held in the afternoon, and I arrived at the Eliseo early. As instructed, I stood in the back of the hall, trying to look as inconspicuous as possible. Fortunately, I immediately ran into Gerardo's girlfriend, Raffaella, who greeted me warmly and suggested we watch the rehearsal together.

A few people began to assemble on the stage, among them Guerrieri. Then, from the front door of the theater by which I had entered, a couple came in: a portly, self-assured man of middle age and a taller, matronly woman in a rather bulky fur coat. They greeted Raffaella warmly, and she introduced me: Signor Battista Meneghini and his wife Maria Meneghini Callas.

I gave the couple a closer look. Both Meneghini and Callas had palpably contented expressions, as if each of them was holding a dearly won prize. Some biographers have implied that the marriage, at least on Callas' side, was dictated by self-interest; but this was surely not the impression they gave at the time. In conversation, in those days, Callas would refer proudly to "my husband the industrialist," and both she and Meneghini were full of little attentions to each other, as if cherishing something precious. For that matter, Maria's letters to Battista, published in his otherwise trivial book, bear out her dependance and devotion.

The fur coat seemed new and expensive. And while we stood there, Callas slipped an enormous ring from her finger and handed it to Raffaella, asking her to take care of it during the rehearsal. For the rest of the afternoon, as we sat in the empty hall, I kept stealing glances at the huge stone – it seemed the size of a calling card – which was whisky-colored (a topaz?) in an elaborate setting. Raffaella was petite: the ring nearly hid her whole finger.

In this Rossini piece, Callas had a comic role; and though, as I later learned, she did not have a great sense of humor offstage, she was perfectly capable of getting laughs when she wanted and when the text allowed them. She played Fiorilla, a termagant Neapolitan wife fascinated by the arrival of a handsome Turkish pasha. On first seeing him, she had to say: "Che bel turco, avviciniamoci" ("What a handsome Turk. Let's move closer"), and in her voice there was just the subtlest hint of a suppressed giggle. Suddenly the quiet matron I had met earlier sounded – and even looked – like a mischievous schoolgirl. Her plumpness also became part of the joke, as the Turks' legendary fondness for ample women was made much of.

One of the artists involved in the little festival was the painter and humorist Mino Maccari, who had designed the costumes. On opening night, I saw them for the first time, with some dismay. They were meant to be funny: bright patches, unmatched trouser-legs, like collages, a kind of thirties avant-garde visual humor that had nothing to do with the refined wit of Felice Romani's delightful libretto. I awaited Callas' entrance with misgivings. Then, to my astonishment, she appeared in a simple 1830s dress of some printed stuff (lawn? calico?) with long sleeves and a prim little white collar. It was totally out of keeping with the rest of the production, but it suited her.

From Raffaella, during the intermission. I heard the story. Maccari had designed for her, too, a comic costume of patches and gaudy colors. She had taken one look, gone to a costumer's and found something vaguely in period (it was actually meant for the second act of *Traviata*) and insisted on wearing it. This was my introduction to her unswerving and unshakeable sense of what was right for her.

It was at about that time that I met Callas again, one evening at Luchino Visconti's villa on the Via Salaria. At the time the house was built by Visconti's father, the area was virtually in the country; and sumptuous though it was, the villa also had a rustic air. Above all, it was superbly run (one imagined a devoted housekeeper, an old family retainer somewhere in the background) and supremely comfortable. One evening, I was invited there for "after dinner." The Meneghinis had clearly dined there, tête-à-tête with Visconti and with the young Franco Zeffirelli, who was living in the villa at the time. I and a few others came in later, for coffee and brandy.

Callas was comfortably sprawled on a shawl-draped sofa, heaped with cushions, very D'Annunzian. Though I didn't know it at the time, this was when the director and soprano were first discussing the possibility of working together. An opera-goer since childhood (his family had been mainstays of La Scala for generations), Visconti had at that time never staged an opera, though he had made films and enjoyed immense – if contested – success in the legitimate theater. Callas, whose Italian career was finally taking off, would be performing at the Florence festival that spring, and in December of 1951 was to inaugurate the season at La Scala.

The after-dinner conversation that evening was a bit stiff. Callas took cordial notice of me because of something I had written about her, and she expressed her appreciation. Zeffirelli, who already harbored ambitions as an opera director himself, had cut from some out-of-town paper a withering review of a young soprano that Callas just might have considered a rival (though it would be like considering June Allyson a rival of Garbo). He read select passages aloud, including one that referred to the artist's "voice of bronze."

"Bronze!" It was the commanding voice of Norma that came from the sofa. "Bronze at least has a sound!"

No one ever incurred Callas' disfavor by speaking ill of another soprano (unless that soprano was dead and enshrined).

Around that time, Callas sang her first Italian *Traviata* in Florence, and – groupie that I now was – I made a special trip up to see it. My new friends Robert Lowell and Elizabeth

Hardwick, after a winter in Rome, were then staying in Florence, and we spent some time sightseeing there together. Lowell came down with a cold, so I took Elizabeth to the *Traviata*. Not an opera-goer, but an acute theater critic, Elizabeth, like me, was carried away. Again, the supporting cast was weak, the production was straight from the warehouse, but Callas shone and provoked tears. The great arias were carried off with panache, every word in the duet with Germont was nuanced, meaningful. But it was in the little moments, the asides, the brief interjections that the artist showed her total immersion in the part. Our eyes became moist, of course, with the great outburst "Amami Alfredo!" but the little phrase, "Ed or si scriva a lui" ("Now I must write to him") as she prepared to compose the final letter to Alfred, really made a shiver of dismay run through the audience.

There are times when even a critic is reluctant to analyze pleasure; and in the intermission before the last act, when I ran into an old friend, the painter Derek Hill, in the foyer of the Comunale and he began to say, "Well, I thought that . . ." I could feel the chill of analysis approaching; and – to Elizabeth's surprise and Derek's – I stammered out, "No, no," turned on my heel, and ran away, to be alone with my complete enchantment. From that evening I have a souvenir, a photograph of Callas in her dressing room, where I went to congratulate her afterwards. It is a terribly unflattering picture (she was not photogenic in her pre-diet days), and I lacked the courage to ask her to sign it; but – though it is an unreliable document – for me it holds some of that night's magic power.

In those days it was hard for me to earn any money in Italy, so I sometimes had to pack up and return to New York where I would get some squalid job, save every possible cent (Chinese restaurants alternated with peanut-butter sandwiches) until I had enough to return to Rome and support myself for a while.

It was during one of these absences that Callas sang her first Scala opening night, a *Vespri Siciliani* that was reported worldwide. But I was back in Italy, and in Milan, for the next year's opening, which finally marked Visconti's operatic debut: *La vestale*, an austere neoclassical work by Spontini, rarely performed (though cherished old Rosa Ponselle 78s had prepared me for the haunting music).

The Milan audience was as elegant as Visconti's simple, grand staging. In the proscenium box, practically on the stage, sat the ancient Toscanini and his daughter Wally, doyenne of Milan society; in another box there was Fosca Crespi, stepdaughter of Puccini, who had married into one of the city's wealthiest industrial families, owners of the then all-powerful *Corriere della Sera*. The audience was full of Visconti admirers, too, and aspiring directors, designers, writers.

During my American absence Callas had gone on a much-reported thinning diet and was now, literally, another person. From inside the buxom, stately matron a glamorous movie star had been released. The dieting had not been entirely a matter of vanity. I remember how, shortly before my departure, I went backstage to congratulate her after a performance. In the course of the action, she had been called upon to kneel down, and – unnoticed by the audience – she had slipped and hit the stage too heavily with her knee. In her direct way, as I was telling her how impressed I was, she pulled up the skirt of her costume and showed me the terrible, unhealthy bruises on her leg. "This happens all the time," she said, and told me she was determined to get rid of the menacing weight.

A day or two after that *Vestale* I had lunch with her at Biffi Scala, to interview her for a magazine. As the magazine was paying, I ordered a full and expensive meal. She had a cup of broth, into which – Greek-style – she squeezed the juice of a lemon, a filet about the size of a silver dollar, some grated raw carrot, then a grated apple for dessert.

From Milan, a little later, Callas came to Rome for a series of perfomances of Cherubini's *Medea*, which she had already sung triumphantly in Florence and at La Scala (conducted by Leonard Bernstein). In Rome, her conductor was not at that level; but the performances – again I attended them all – were searing. At her first appearance, veiled, she seized the attention of the audience (and the Roman audience, composed to some extent of politicians, is never the most alert); and when, asked to identify herself, she lifted the veil and sang simply, "Medea," the familiar chill ran down everyone's spine.

During this run of performances, I gave a little party for her. At that time I was sharing a fairly large apartment with an aristocratic young friend of Visconti's, Ruggero Nuvolari; and between the two of us, we assembled an impressive guest list. I invited much of the Anglo-American colony: Iris Tree; Jennie Cross (Robert Graves's daughter) and her husband Patrick, head of the Reuters bureau; John and Virginia Becker (whose parties in Palazzo Caetani were a focal point for the foreign residents of Rome). Luchino came with his entourage. Ruggero invited various members of the aristocracy, included the delightful but formidable Roman hostess Countess Mimi Pecci Blunt, who brought as her escort an ancient Sicilian nobleman, the Principe Belmonte.

The apartment was spacious and, thanks to the previous tenant from whom we sublet, well furnished. It had one drawback. It was on the top floor and there was no elevator. As some of the younger guests arrived they would announce the progress of the less young (fortunately there were benches on the landings). "Mimi and the Prince are on the third floor," a guest would inform us, and a short time later we would learn that they had progressed to the fourth.

One of the Americans I had invited was Ned Rorem. He was in fact the first to arrive. At that time, Ned was an on-and-off alcoholic. My heart sank when he said, "I think I'll have a martini." Ned drunk was as dire a guest as Ned, sober, was enchanting. Fortunately like my heart, Ned also sank; and within minutes, he had been safely put to bed in my room, unconscious. I locked the door, just in case; but he didn't come around until the party was safely over. His Rome diaries tell the story a bit differently, but in this instance I trust my memory more than his (I stuck to wine).

Maria herself, among the last to appear, seemed unfazed by the stairs and was in great, regal form. She wore a dull-gold tailleur with mink collar and cuffs, stood squarely in the center of the room and let the party circle around her. My friend John Becker, who had injured his ankle skiing and had a leg in a cast, made a rueful remark about his struggle up to the party, just to pay homage to her. He expected some polite recognition of his efforts, but Maria merely nodded and smiled serenely, as if those efforts were no more than her due. Similarly, when I once told her I had made a trip all the way to Verona to hear her in *Mefistofele* and had heard only half a dozen notes from her before being rained out, her frank and unconsoling reply was: "Oh yes, I remember that night: easiest money I ever made."

The 1954-55 season at La Scala was the great Visconti-Callas season, and *La Vestale* was followed, a few months later, by *La Sonnambula*. This Bellini work, till then rather neglected, was subsequently interpreted by other sopranos, including Joan Sutherland; some American critics have called the work boring. All I can say is that, with Callas, with Bernstein conducting and Visconti staging (and with a cast that also included Valletti), only a deaf and blind man could have been bored.

I reached Milan in time for some of the rehearsals, and in time also to get a taste of pre-opening tension. Callas' success, which was now assuming celebrity proportions, had aroused the predictable amount of envy and hostility along with excited anticipation; and the Milanese public was sharply divided into pro and anti factions. Days before the opening night of *Sonnambula* the whole city seemed to be choosing sides. For many non-Milanese Italians and for the foreigners who know the city only superficially, Milan has a reputation for being cold, commercial, a place where the men think only of money and the women think only of men (with money). But this description of Milan is false today and, forty years ago, it was even further from reality.

When you visit Milan you quickly realize that the opera house, the Teatro alla Scala, is – literally, physically – the heart of the city. For over two centuries it has stood directly opposite the Palazzo Marino, the city hall, which is flanked by the main office of the Banca Commerciale on one side, and the Gallery on the other. Banking, politics, commerce, social life are essential parts of the city's focus; but La Scala dominates them all. It is no accident that after the war, one of the first buildings to be rebuilt in Milan was La Scala. The Palazzo Marino, also war-damaged, had to wait much longer.

And the Scala audience of the Callas years was the same audience that had applauded the return of Arturo Toscanini from political exile to conduct the first concert in the reopened house. It was a mettlesome audience, ready to express its likes and dislikes. Visconti was a son of Milan, but that was no guarantee of uncritical acceptance. Callas was an outsider and, as far as the Scala was concerned, she seemed to have at least temporarily unseated Tebaldi, who, if not Milanese, came from the Parma area, the birthplace of Verdi and Toscanini.

La Sonnambula tells the story of a simple village girl, Amina, who is loved, then misguidedly rejected, then loved again by a young local landowner. Visconti decided that, with Callas at his disposal, the image of the simple village girl could be boldly revised. In the first act, true, she was dressed for her betrothal ceremony in an unassuming white dress designed by Piero Tosi, with a wreath of flowers circling her head. But in the last act, when love triumphs, Visconti decided that Callas, imitating the behavior of any self-respecting prima donna of the nineteenth century (whose style he was recreating), would bedeck herself with her grandest jewels: and, as she sang the ecstatic coloratura of the final number, the house lights would gradually be brought up until, on the last, ringing note, the great chandelier would blaze forth, and La Scala – jewels on the stage, in the boxes, and the orchestra seats – would be all asparkle.

It was a risk, and could have fallen flat; but instead, it triumphed, and even the scattered catcalls of the diehard Tebaldians could not mar the occasion. Callas, as I recall, appeared only briefly at the supper party given afterwards at Toscanini's house (the maestro had gone to bed before the guests arrived), where I met Bernstein for the first time and had a long talk with him about Bellini's recitatives (I realized later that Lenny had that great gift of becoming sincerely interested in the interests of his interlocutors). It was not a large party, but it collected all of musical Milan, in those rooms where since the early years of the century the maestro had talked and rehearsed with singers and composers. The shades of Boito, Puccini, and countless others hovered over us.

That was a rich season at La Scala, but unfortunately not a rich one for me, so I was unable to attend the opening night of the Visconti-Callas *Traviata*, where the tension was even higher and the hostility even greater (that was the occasion when an enemy threw Callas a bunch of radishes, which the nearsighted soprano mistook for rosebud and kissed with a winning smile).

After scraping up some cash, I came to a later, calmer, but no less exciting performance. Visconti shifted the setting from the 1850s Paris of Dumas fils to the later, harsher Paris of Zola, and Violetta's sitting room, with its paisley throws, its dark red walls, its huge cushions, its ornate fireplace bore a certain resemblance to Visconti's villa on the Via Salaria. At the end of the party, left alone, Visconti's Violetta kicked off her shoes with relief and sang her great solo aria in her stockinged feet. Even at the performance I attended, the audience emitted a collective gasp of shock, before Callas' singing silenced them.

I went to the performance, with my old friend Elliott Stein, who had come down from Paris for the event. Like me, he had procured a photograph of the diva – we both had chosen the same, superb moment in the second act, when Violetta reacts, head held high, to her public humiliation by Alfredo – and after the final curtain, I took Elliott to Maria's dressing-room, to introduce him and to have her sign our photographs. It had been a good performance, and she was in high spirits, charming, talkative. But when I brought out the photographs, she waved them away. "No, no. Bill," she said, "come to the house for coffee tomorrow after lunch and I'll give you a better one." Elliott was clearly not included in the invitation.

I arrived punctually at the recently acquired Meneghini house near the Piazza Buonarroti, a modern villa of several stories, small but luxurious, the rooms I saw furnished in sound, anonymous taste, neither vulgar nor individual. The Meneghinis had finished lunch and were in the living room on the second floor. Coffee was served; I politely declined a cognac (the label betrayed its Italian origin, and even in my relative poverty I had learned to avoid cheap Italian brandy). Then Battista vanished to his study upstairs, and Maria and I talked.

One of the most debated (and booed) features of Visconti's staging of *La Traviata* was the death scene. Violetta, in her apparent recovery, wants to rush to church: she throws a shawl around her nightdress, puts on her hat, but suddenly her briefly regained strength fails, she sinks into a wing chair, and dies. With her hat on. The conservative Milanesi were already outraged that she should die in a chair, instead of slumping to the floor in the traditional dramatic faint; but that Visconti should make her die with a bonnet on her head, its strings loose at her throat, was too much.

By the time I saw the production, Visconti had left Milan for Rome, and Callas had discreetly revised this scene. She did put the hat on, she did die seated, but somehow between those two moments, the hat somehow slipped off her head, and her long, lustrous hair fell romantically around her shoulders. Callas, like many of Visconti's closest friends, called him not by the diminutive Luchino, but by his birth-certificate name. She said: "Luca knows nothing about how women dress. The hat is the very last thing you put on before leaving the house. Violetta wouldn't have got that far . . ."

After some more talk about the performance and her future plans, I reminded her of the photographs she had promised, the real reason for my visit. "Oh yes," she said, and picking up the phone, she dialed her husband's extension, obviously showing off this new gadget. A moment later, the butler appeared with a photograph. It was not, to my dismay, a scene from Traviata, but a studio portrait by a fashionable Milanese photographer. The new, slim Callas was seen in a smart dress, probably designed by her friend Biki (step granddaughter of Puccini), with a simple stole, a foolish little hat, gloves, a bracelet over the right glove, a stupendous but discreet necklace, earrings. The great eyes are looking just over the camera, not quite at the viewer, the full lips are almost pouting, the eyebrows are unplucked, but accented. It is a splendid photograph of a remarkable-looking woman, but despite the autograph "Maria Meneghini Callas," as she then insisted on being billed, it still is not the Callas I knew. On stage, even if larger than life, Callas always seemed real, natural; here, in reality, she is posed, an impressive artifact.

Suddenly, I remembered poor Elliott, defrauded of his photograph, too, and though Callas clearly was expecting her next visitor, I mustered my courage and mentioned the friend I had presented to her last night. Again, she picked up the phone. "Titta, send down another picture," she said. Then, as her frugality took over, she added: "A small one."

So I have the big, studio portrait in full fig; Elliott has a postcard picture of Callas, also in street clothes but less formal, a hand almost saucily on one hip, to emphasize her new waistline.

Two things always impressed me about Callas in those great years: her total seriousness about her work, which meant punctuality, thorough preparation of a role and irate impatience with any colleague who had been lazy about studying a part; and, along with this, her honesty about her own singing. "Oh, why did you have to come tonight?" she would say to me, if I turned up in her dressing-room after a performance she considered less than her best. (I might add she would say the same thing if some colleague had not been at *his* best. "Did you hear how he clung to that C for dear life?")

Then, tragically, the voice began to go. It was still possible to hear and enjoy a performance – her Scala *Poliuto*, for example – even after her decline began; but then, at a certain point, a Callas evening could be embarrassing, painful, a lot had to be taken on faith. In December of 1961 I took a non-operatic friend, the Italian novelist Luigi Malerba, to La Scala to a Callas *Medea*. Convinced this would be the ideal introduction for an operatically ignorant intellectual, I waited eagerly for the entrance, for the self-identifying "Medea" to overwhelm my companion; the scene came and it fell flat. The word sounded weak, insignificant. The whole interpretation was lackluster, almost hesitant. But the Scala audience was now studded with Callas' musically ignorant, jet-set friends (she had shed Meneghini, both in her billing and in her life, and was photographed everywhere with Onassis), who applauded and cheered, no matter what.

At the end I really didn't want to go to the dressing room, but I had promised Malerba to introduce him, and Callas knew I was in the house. As we started across the stage, I saw that Callas had been held there by a swarm of fans. Ahead of us, directed towards her, was the imposing bulk of the Begum, who gave Maria an occlusive hug, saying, "Maria, you were sublime."

I waited for Callas to demur, as she would have done in the past, but, to my surprise and disappointment, I heard her say, "Yes, I thought I sang well this evening."

Apologizing to Malerba, I turned and led him to the stage door, out of the house, and to the Commendatore's bar on the corner of the square.

After that *Medea* she sang no opera for over a year, limiting her activity to a few concerts and some recordings. Then, in January of 1964, the miracle occurred: a new production of *Tosca* was mounted for her at the Royal Opera House in Covent Garden, and somehow – through a sixth sense opera-lovers possess – word spread that this was going to be an occasion. And the opening night audience was not only glittering, but also dedicated. Many of the international set were present, inevitably, but so were the truly devoted. I heard Italian spoken everywhere in the foyer, in the Crush Bar. The electricity in the air reminded me of the great Scala openings of a decade earlier.

Zeffirelli's production – nothing like the vulgar super-spectacles he devises nowadays – was beautiful and true. Callas' entrance was not the stately progress of a crook-carrying diva, as in old-fashioned productions, but the feline spring of a jealous young woman, eyes nervously searching for a hidden rival. The tenor Renato Cioni had youth and sincerity on his side, and an impassioned if not perfectly controlled voice. As the wicked Scarpia, Tito Gobbi, Callas' co-star in dozens of performances, equalled her intensity and commitment. The miracle, to be honest, was actually a *near*-miracle: Callas' voice was not what it had been, but still it was thrilling, and in Tosca the vitality of an interpretation can compensate for occasional vocal harshness.

In the first intermission I ran into Wally Toscanini (it really was like being at La Scala), and we exchanged greetings. "I was so afraid I wouldn't be able to make it," the Countess said. "Emanuela's father was very ill . . . Emanuela was Wally's daughter and her father was Count Castelbarco, Wally's long-separated but never-divorced husband. "Of course, he was *very* old. And he was sick for a long time . . ." Then, after a dutiful sigh, she blurted: "I thought he'd *never* die." Fortunately, he died in time for the funeral to be held and for his widow to fly to London for the opening.

The following spring, after a long absence, Callas returned to the Metropolitan for two *Tosca*s. Then, when she was back in Paris I received a call from Geraldine Souvaine, legendary, outspoken producer of the Texaco broadcasts, asking me to go to Paris and record an interview with Callas, who had agreed to the taping provided the questions were submitted to her in advance. Souvaine and Edward Downes had written the questions and cleared them with her. I set off for Paris, where a copy of the questions was awaiting me.

On arrival, I was to call the Paris office of EMI to find out the time of the taping, which would take place in Callas' apartment near the Étoile. Barely off the tram, I called. Callas, an assistant told me, had a slight cold and could not receive me that day. I was to call back tomorrow at noon. The cold persisted. Each day I was asked to call again at mid-day tomorrow. Thus it was hard for me to make plans or enjoy Paris, also because every night I had to call New York to report to the short-tempered Geraldine, whose usual recommendation was on the order of "tell that bitch to shit or get off the pot." Geraldine's suggestions evoked unspeakable scenes.

By the time the hour was fixed – 3 P.M. – I was in a state of mind-splitting agitation. I lunched with some Americans-in-Paris friends – John Ashbery and Harry Matthews were in the group – and tried to limit my consumption of wine. As I set off for the appointment John gave me a reassuring pill to take. I arrived at the apartment so thoroughly reassured that I could have interviewed Hitler without a qualm.

The faithful Bruna, whom I knew from Milan, admitted me with a smile of recognition and led me into the bedroom, where Callas was lying in state, the picture of health. EMI had set up enough equipment to tape the last act of *Carmen*. I was given a seat beside the bed and I spread out the pages of questions in front of me, propping them against Callas' right thigh. Someone gave us a signal and we started talking.

I don't remember the interview very well (and it would sadden me to listen to it now, even if I had a tape); but I remember that we very quickly strayed from the set questions and simply conversed. We talked about the differences between Greece and Crete (because of Medea), about the possibility of her acting in plays (she was dubious). From time to time my eyes would stray curiously to the little silver frame on the bedside table; I recognized a smiling Onassis. In due course, I took my leave.

"Be sure to call whenever you're in Paris," she said warmly, as if I hadn't been trying regularly for days to see her.

Shortly after that meeting, she made a few more attempts at opera, interrupted a performance of *Norma* at the Paris Opera, and sang a final, reluctant, politely received *Tosca* at Covent Garden. For several years, I followed her life only through the newspapers, the gossip columns more often than the music page. Her return to the concert stage was announced: partnered by the tenor Giuseppe Di Stefano, her one-time leading man, whose voice was now in even more parlous state than hers, she was to give joint recitals all over the world. The reports were so disastrous, the cancellations so frequent that, even when I was invited to attend one of the recitals, I declined. I was happy that my last memory of her as a performer was that London *Tosca*; I did not want to spoil it.

But we met finally on one other occasion. The Chicago Lyric Opera, with the support of some Chicago patrons, sponsored an international conference of Verdi studies, at which I and many musicologist friends were invited to speak. And Callas, who was to he in the city at the time, agreed to participate in a roundtable discussion of Verdi one afternoon. The roundtable consisted of the late Mario Medici, head of the Verdi Institute in Parma (who spoke no English), Callas, and me. In effect, I was to be the moderator.

On the day of the event Carol Fox, dynamic head of the Lyric Opera, invited me to lunch with Callas, Di Stefano, and Medici. It was a lighthearted occasion. The two singers were resting before another leg of their tour (I believe it meant a trip to Japan), and though their quarrels had been widely reported, at this lunch Di Stefano had found an affectionate, teasing tone that kept Callas in a good humor. As usual, she ate a frugal lunch (shrimp cocktail with lemon juice and no tomato sauce, a steak, a salad). The waiter came for dessert orders, and Di Stefano immediately announced he wanted a chocolate sundae; with the air of someone who has discovered a jealously guarded gastronomic secret, he successfully urged Medici to have one, too. Then he insisted with Callas, who virtuously said no several times, shaking her head as if in horror, until she finally murmured, "Not chocolate. Butterscotch." Then she added, in reparation, "Bill will help me."

The butterscotch sundae was placed in front of her. Primly, she took the tiniest spoonful and made a great show of pushing the dish over to me, at her left. A near-diabetic, I am forbidden sweets, so I also took only a token spoonful, but I left the dish where it was. As the lively conversation flowed around us, I saw a quasi-surreptitious hand move toward me, then those expressive, tapering fingers slowly drew the dish away and, without another word, the sundae was consumed.

The discussion later that day had its moments of interest, but even more, its moments of hilarity. The most significant question concerned cuts in Verdi's operas. Asked to comment on them – to an audience largely of serious scholars, musical purists – Callas said blithely, "Oh, they don't cut nearly enough." One scholar wanted an example; her reply was prompt: "Why, the baritone aria in *Traviata*. It's so boring, and it goes on and on." It was noticed that she didn't suggest any reduction of Verdi's soprano parts. To conclude, she said, "I nearly died when I read how some scholars had found even *more* music for *Don Carlos*. The opera is far too long already."

I looked at the front row of the little theater and saw the three scholars chiefly responsible for the addition of another half hour of music to *Don Carlos*: Ursula Gunther, David Rosen, and Andrew Porter. Three tactfully blank faces.

I felt that, for once, Verdi needed a spokesman, so I said hesitantly: "Mme. Callas, if I may disagree with you . . ."

"You have a right to disagree with me, Mr. Weaver," she said with imperious generosity.

I couldn't help myself. "I know I have the right," I said curtly. "I'm not sure I have the nerve."

The audience forgot about tact and laughed uproariously. Fortunately, she laughed too. And the roundtable ended in great good humor.

Callas had asked Miss Fox for protection from fans, so the security around the dressing room was very tight. As the hall was emptying, I went and knocked on the door and was bidden to come in. Security had been so completely successful that not a soul had got in to see the star; and, unused to such neglect – the discussion had, after all, been a kind of performance – Callas was sitting there, her expression half puzzled and half grumpy. Luckily, at that moment, someone from the press office came in with a stack of photographs, asking her to sign them for patrons and members of the house staff. Delighted to have something to do, Callas set to work at once, scrupulously inscribing each photograph. Murmuring a goodbye, I left her to her task.

I never saw her again. On the rare occasions when I passed through Paris in the remaining years of her life, I thought of her invitation to call her, but I no longer had her number, and somehow – again – my nerve failed.

In September of 1977, with my friend Andrew Porter (who has a house in Tuscany near mine), I went to a small town in the Veneto to hear and review a rare opera. We had arranged to hire a car the next morning and were planning to spend a few days driving around an area neither of us knew very well. The performance was dismal and, during the night, there was a gargantuan thunderstorm. I was kept awake by howling winds, lashing bursts of rain, the sound of boughs being ripped off old trees. (I learned later that we were at the edge of a severe earthquake that destroyed whole towns in the Friuli region.) Having slept hardly at all, I got up early and was writing my review when Andrew came into the room. "Maria is dead," he announced, having just heard the news on the radio. "Let's go home." We canceled the car, paid our hotel bill, and took the first train back to Tuscany. An era in our lives – and in the history of music – had ended.

FROM FLORENCE INTO HISTORY

Alfredo Mandelli

A new period in musical history will be known as A.C. *After Callas*, like the *After Wagner* and *After Toscanini*. Where and when did it all start and how did it happen? Looking carefully at the facts and with a liberal helping of reflection, the moment and the place can be found. This is naturally conditioned by B.C., *Before Callas*, a *Before* that called herself Maria Sofia Kalogeropoulos who was later to become Maria Callas.

The Maria Callas phenomenon is part of the musical history of Opera and the other phenomenon known as music, forever changing though always remaining the same. It is a moment that lasts but a few years, the place, seen at the center of a circle, along the edges are first Verona, then Venice, the center is Florence; from there the circle expands to include Milan. The moment is from 1948 to 1953.

August 1947, *La Gioconda* is being broadcast on the radio from the arena of Verona. Famous names are taking part starting with Tullio Serafin and the American tenor Richard Tucker, Elena Nicolai, Tagliabue, and Rossi-Lemeni. The only *unknown* is the lead: Maria Callas. Curiously enough that name already had an important ring to it.

I was listening to the broadcast with my father, a musician with high standards and a formidable opinion on vocal technique. He despised the pushed and throttled sounds of some singers along with the *gigionate* (hamming it up) and the off-hand approach to the technical side of singing. The much-admired examples were Pertile, Toscanini, Guarnieri and De

Sabata. Callas: What would she be like? Not all was perfect; even so what was most notable was her extraordinary determination. The fact that she had been engaged was unusual, as singing in the Arena was an honor reserved for artists with major career experience. This unknown singer, uneven, but using an impressive vocal palette and a sense of domination carried herself with honor in that melodrama *par excellence, La Gioconda*.

Our belief was that we would soon be hearing more about this *unknown*. Only a few months later we read that this *unknown* had sung *Isolde* in Venice, again conducted by Serafin. Wagner: No joke. The search was on for even more roles. After all, Callas had studied with Elvira De Hidalgo who had specialized in coloratura roles. The *Norma* of November 1948 at the Teatro Comunale of Florence (not the present building but the Politeama known affectionately as *Il Fiorentino*, with tiers of stone and a glass roof) was the turning point. This theatre was the headquarters of the *Maggio Musicale* started in 1933 by Vittorio Gui.

Gui was interested in presenting works outside the standard repertoire and Siciliani's choice, as artistic director of the festival, must undoubtedly have pleased him. Finding himself able to use the talent and startling versatility of Callas was indeed good fortune; he had understood where others, such as La Scala, had ignored her or in other cases for various reasons had not accepted her.

Although the contracts had started to come in from a variety of sources, the *Maggio* was able to claim the right to having crowned Callas before her triumphs at La Scala. Florence proved to be the ideal place for the making of a new artist whose unique ability was to accentuate that which often had been trivialized and cheapened in this repertoire even when clothed in a luxurious production and performed by other important singers.

Callas, while contributing a new and intense *modern* reading of operas cherished by everyone, brought the values and standards of the Bel Canto and post Bel Canto periods to light simply by singing every note written. She did not try to emulate the singers of the nineteenth century nor try to find impossible accuracy as was later to become the illusory quest of some (one of the distorted consequences of the *After Callas* period), but achieved a balance between original authenticity and the reactions of the contemporary listener.

This meant revitalizing the known repertoire as well as representing older works that had been forgotten, allowing them to be performed and proving just how much they were still of interest. It seemed impossible to Siciliani that this girl should return to America without contracts and the means to live after hearing the qualities she had displayed and he had discovered. It was Siciliani who on hearing her understood that with Maria Callas, the dramatic coloratura soprano of a hundred years ago (before Bel Canto had passed out of fashion) had been reborn.

In between the *Isoldes*, the *Kundrys*, the *Turandots* and the *Aidas*, Serafin could sense that there was something more. His vision was that which Callas was to become. The Florentine festival where Siciliani had just taken the helm proved to be the ideal setting for this renaissance. In her he had found musicality, professionalism, dramatic understanding and a potential actress. Florence and Francesco Siciliani; seldom has a match been so auspicious and balanced between theater and artist.

A production of *Traviata* preceded Callas' *Norma* in Florence: her interpretation of this work had a more shocking effect than the Bellini work. In the modernism of this interpretation of Verdi's Violetta, the true artist had been found. Meanwhile Serafin had announced the latest and most astounding revelation of what Callas was capable of: The role of Elvira in *I Puritani*, to be sung during the same period that she was singing the *Walkyrie* at the Fenice in Venice.

Maria Callas' first real work with the *Maggio Musicale* was in 1951 singing *I Vespri Siciliani* conducted by Erich Kleiber. Siciliani's genius was inserting this rarely performed work into the program of revived operas and the lesser-known works of Verdi and having them conducted by the great symphonic conductors.

During the same festival, the professionalism of Callas was applied to a work of Haydn. World renowned for his symphonies and chamber works, and almost entirely unknown as a composer of Opera, his *Orfeo and Euridice* was performed, again conducted by Kleiber. Within days she also gave a recital at the Grand Hotel with Bruno Bartoletti at the piano gave vent to her vocal pyrotechnics in the forgotten but once famous *Proch Variations* and created stereophonic echo effects in the Ombra Leggera from Mayerbeer's opera *Dinorah*.

Florence also had a Callas *Puritani* with Eugene Conley and conducted by Serafin before the next festival in 1952 when Siciliani experimented with a Rossini "serio," *Armida,* till then regarded as a Belcanto opera of no particular significance.

Back in Milan and at La Scala, something had stirred on the wave of her success, also due to the interest expressed by Arturo Toscanini. Better late than never. It was said he didn't like her singing and there was talk of *aceto nella voce* (vinegar in her voice). Toscanini may well have said that but certain phrases are often repeated out of context, in particular those uttered by the maestro about singers possibly caused by his noted love-hate relationship with this category. As such, his "Well, well . . ." for Gigli could have had a thousand meanings; also his saying *The voice of an angel* about Tebaldi, chosen by him for the reopening of La Scala after the restoration of World War II bomb damage.

Rumor has it that he was only referring to the part of an angel she sang in an audition. (The opinion of Giorgio Gualerzi, most likely remembering that she had sung the part of the Celestial voice in Refice's *Cecilia*.) After all he had used the same phrase on hearing Rosetta Pampanini rehearsing *Butterfly* at La Scala in 1925. This time he was not looking for angels but a Lady Macbeth, a creature from hell; at eighty-four years of age he was planning to conduct *Macbeth* (at Busseto as he had done with Falstaff) and was unable to find a suitable *Lady Macbeth*.

He accompanied Callas in the part and decided that she was right for it. Unfortunately the years had taken their toll and he deferred. It was an encounter destined to take place between two reformists of repertoire and artistic custom.

Callas performed *Lady Macbeth* in 1952 at La Scala under the thrilling direction of De Sabata and caused shivers in the banquet scene with her use of the words "Voi siete demente," the same words that had so impressed Toscanini. After a *Lucia*, also recorded on LP, the Maggio Musicale's next opera was *Medea* by Cherubini. Giulio Confalonieri who had been involved in a campaign to revive the works of Cherubini, until recently almost forgotten in Italy, could now see his labors bear fruit. Vittorio Gui came down from his hilltop retreat in Fiesole and conducted the *Medea*. He had been a staunch ally in a spectacular performance of *Nabucco* at the San Carlo Opera house in Naples and he was thrilled to find himself working with someone capable of bringing the necessary fire to Cherubini's masterpiece. Only a few months later *Medea* thrilled La Scala audiences where Callas was even more fiery under the baton of the young Leonard Bernstein.

Florence had paved the way to La Scala. There was stubborn dissent however the infamous and ironic "Euh, bella voce!" during the lesson scene in the *Barber of Seville* preserved for posterity on the live recording; likewise the "Euh, bella musica!" referring to Richard Strauss's *Rosenkavalier* in 1911 and again to Stravinsky's *Petrouchka* also at La Scala where someone shouted the phrase *Fiera di Porta Genova*! (referring to the flea market at the northern gate of Milan).

Whenever a *breakaway* artist like Callas arrives on the scene there are always rumors, sensational revelations and avalanches of *news* surrounding everything the artist does. Stories, generally without any sense, including the so-called rivalries are futile when aimed at the inimitable phenomenon that she is. All documentation, the accounts, the behind-the-scenes chattering, be they true or false, help us to understand the myth of the diva and not only the historical facts, but that of a human drama after which the post-Callas period was born.

THE MEMOIRS OF A VENETIAN FRIEND

Pucci Anfodillo

"Maria, if only they knew how good you are, they'd love you even more." These were the words used by Victor De Sabata to a young Callas in the early fifties after having conducted her unforgettable performances of *Vespri Siciliani, Tosca* and *Macbeth*. Other than the obvious and clear meaning of these words, what was he alluding to?

These words came to mind when I had the good fortune to meet Maria Callas through my father, a friend of Meneghini; perhaps because I was very young and my own obsession for music made me the willing devotee of maestro De Sabata. The adoration I felt towards this unparalleled artist was exclusive over and above any other of the great singers. In the beginning Callas was not liked, and left the regular theatergoers bewildered. This was both due to her choice of repertoire and her interpretation of the roles. I remember her meticulous attention to a composer's requirements and having absolute faith in finding everything in the music that would be essential to the correct interpretation of the role.

During the time she sang at the Arena of Verona and at the Fenice, I remember the subject of her conversations always being about the character she was performing both past and present: No, the singer that visited us in our home was not yet the queen of the Jet Set and with great simplicity she combined the superb results of her work with the hard work and commitment of an athlete.

During the mad scene in a *Lucia* at the Fenice, when one of the high notes did not work out, she resolved it by taking a lower alternative note. Later visiting her in her dressing room she did not seem very unhappy about it, knowing that her interpretation of this tragic heroine went beyond sterile technical perfection, something that she had never followed to the letter. She told me that to sing with agility, all the notes must be sung as real notes and at full voice but they should also be expressive and blend into the madness which she had made her own.

While talking about agility, I recall that Rudolf Bing of the Metropolitan Opera in New York had the inspiration to ask her to sing the role of the Queen of the Night in Mozart's *Magic Flute*. Nothing came of it but I can't help wondering what she might have done with this brilliant role. Another project, which alas, came to nothing, was to sing the role of Leonora in *Il Trovatore* for the opening scene of Luchino Visconti's film *Senso*. Due to prior engagements she was unable to be in Venice during the shooting of the film, Visconti later directed her in many unforgettable performances but, in my opinion, did not add much to her growth as an actress as she was at an early age quite capable of being the center of attention on stage.

The triumphal scene during an *Aida* at the Arena of Verona stands out in my memory. *Aida*, the captive slave, certainly not the focal point of the scene, held me enthralled and with a few simple gestures and glances communicated all of her grief in seeing both her past and her future pass in front of her. I believe I was not the only person to be watching her even in moments of silence.

For me the supreme moment was a *Norma* at La Scala in 1955 that Callas had invited me to see. In the last act, after the prayer to her father, *Norma* made her way with brief but firm steps to the sacrificial altar under a long black veil. The emotion in the theatre was palpable: I'm sure at that moment we would all have willingly followed her to the sacrifice to experience again a new innocence wrapped in that veil, like Wagner in the black sails of *Tristan*. A long silence followed the ringing down of the curtain and then came the applause, a real explosion.

I believe that when music and theatre yield emotions as strong as these, they become part of us and memory and regret merge to become everlasting.

MARIA CALLAS

Anita Pensotti

When I met Maria Callas many years ago, she liked to be called Maria Meneghini Callas out of affection and devotion to her husband; critics were still guarded about her voice calling it a *rebus* or *tricolor* but she was by now famous. So famous that her husband *Commendator* Meneghini would often be astonished and exclaim on returning with her from their travels (she in first class; he in tourist). "Do you know, so many of the passengers recognized Maria?"

Time magazine had done an extensive article on her in Italy, Greece and the U.S.A. The author of the article after an unprecedented two hours with her during which she answered all questions, even the most insidious with her usual bluntness, had undertaken as a favor to go to Rome and pick up a toy poodle, a gift from an admirer and take it to Milan.

The poodle's name was Toy and I remember clearly seeing it in her arms where she would caress it repeatedly and talk to it like a baby. "So much cuddling," Meneghini would say with a touch of jealousy. Irritated she would respond: "Whom should I be cuddling? My colleagues?"

It was the moment of the great makeover of Maria Kalogeropoulos into a slim, sophisticated and bejeweled star, born in New York to Greek parents and married to an Italian, the Veronese business man Titta Meneghini who had made his money in the production of bricks.

The meeting with the two leaders of Ambrosian chic, Luchino Visconti and Biki, was a seminal factor in her new look and regrettably also in the decline of her vocal chords. Biki did not beat about the bush with Maria when she went to her atelier to order some gowns.

"How much do you weigh? More than a *quintale* (100 kilograms)?" "Before returning to me you must lose weight as fast as possible," she said to her glaring at her plump and ungainly body. "At least thirty kilos; no less." Visconti who directed her in *La Traviata* explained to her that Margherita Gualtier dies of consumption and therefore has to be fragile, delicate, more than a flower . . . As we all know, Maria obeyed. How did she do it?

Much has been speculated about her celebrated weight loss and I can tell you with certainty that the instrument of this impressive feat was a rapacious tape worm swallowed with an iron will in a glass of champagne. I know that something as revolting as this intrusive parasite is hardly compatible with the everyday life of a diva but that's what happened. Maria Callas and her husband never had any reservations about confessing the truth to me. In the months that I visited them in Via Buonarotti, Callas closely followed the maintenance program set out for her by her doctors.

I remember her sitting at the dining table lining up chocolates given to her by a friend just for fun, or offering me a dish of delicious piece of Loukum saying, "Anita, please take one, I can't eat them . . ." To the end of her days she was meticulous about food and alcohol but I am told that later in Paris she would get up late at night and tiptoe into the kitchen and open the refrigerator door.

Maria asked me to do her a favor: to do my work with her from eleven PM onwards. "I have to go to bed late," she told me, "or else I can't get to sleep and stay awake for hours." So I started what I light-heartedly called my Callassian nights, nights that were frequent and allowed me to get to know Callas

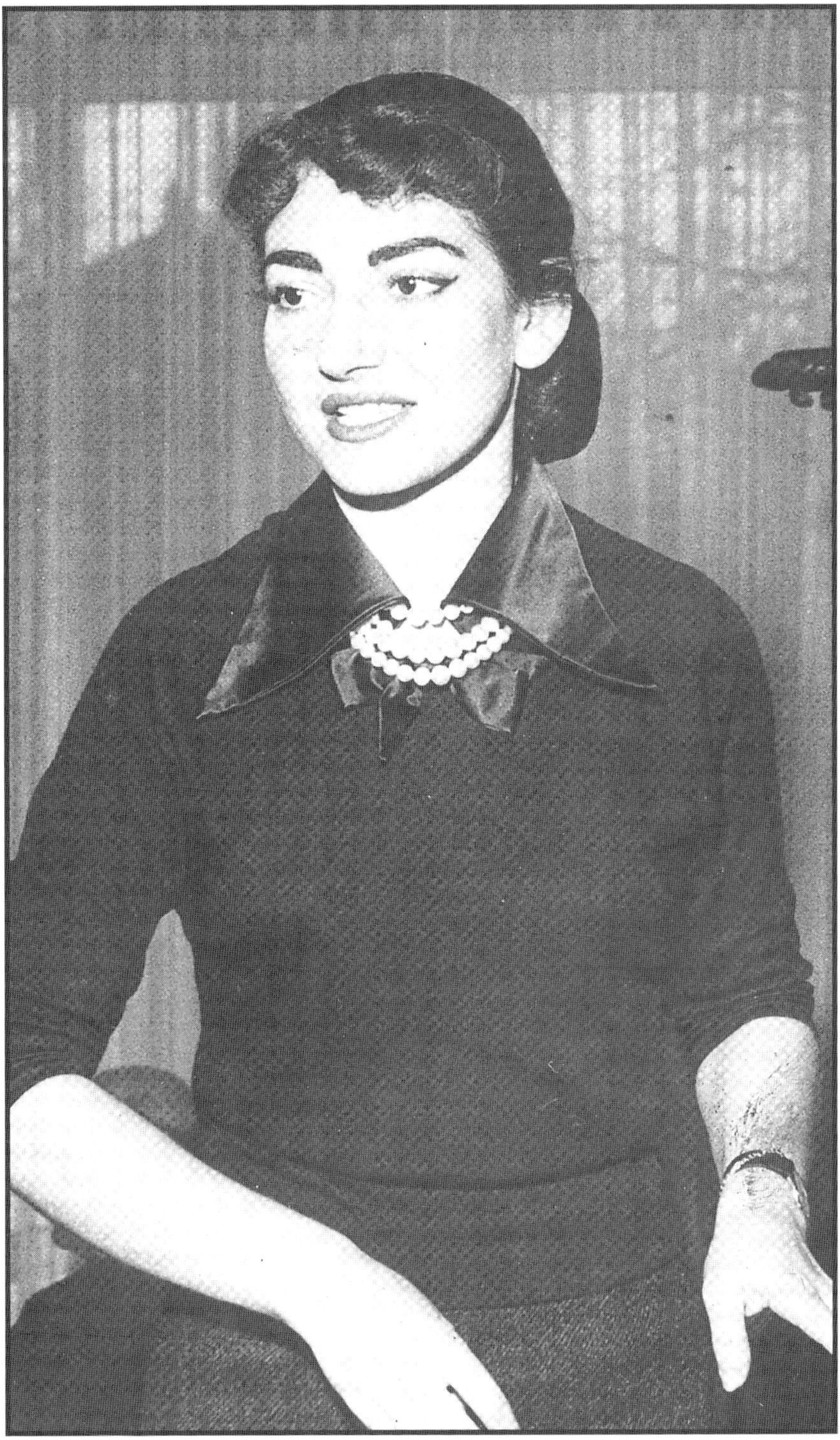

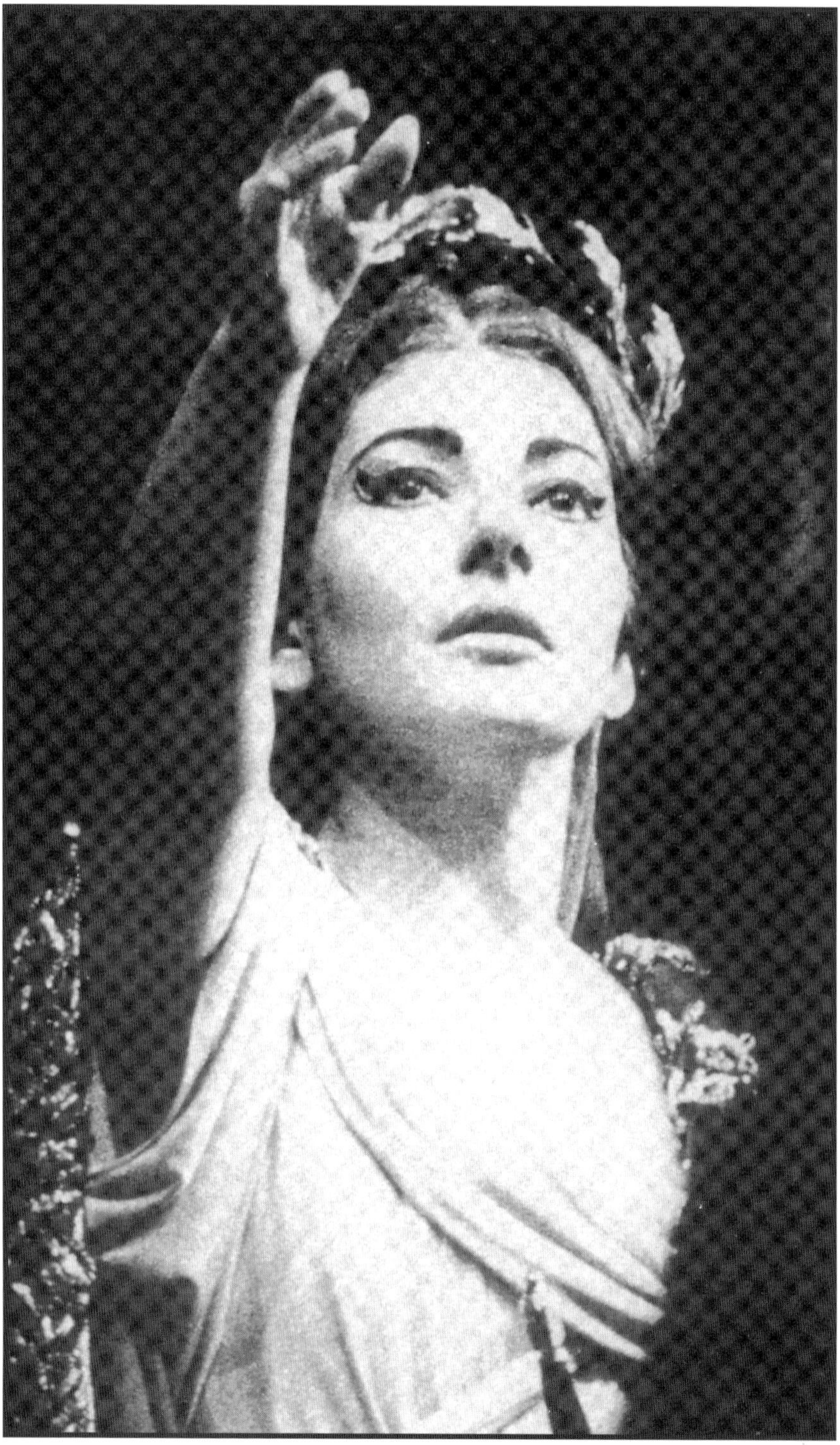

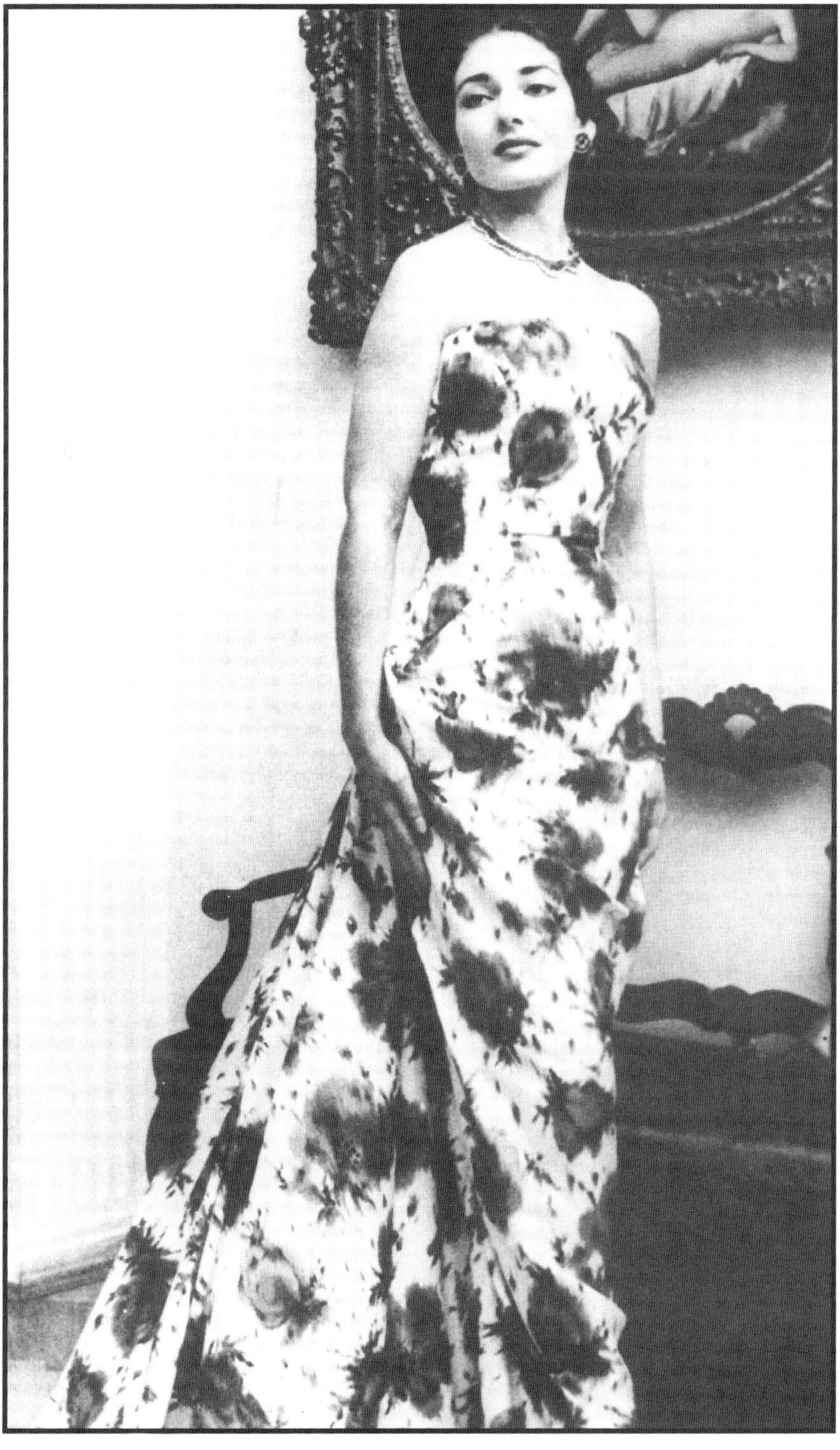

Medea - Scala di Milano 1953

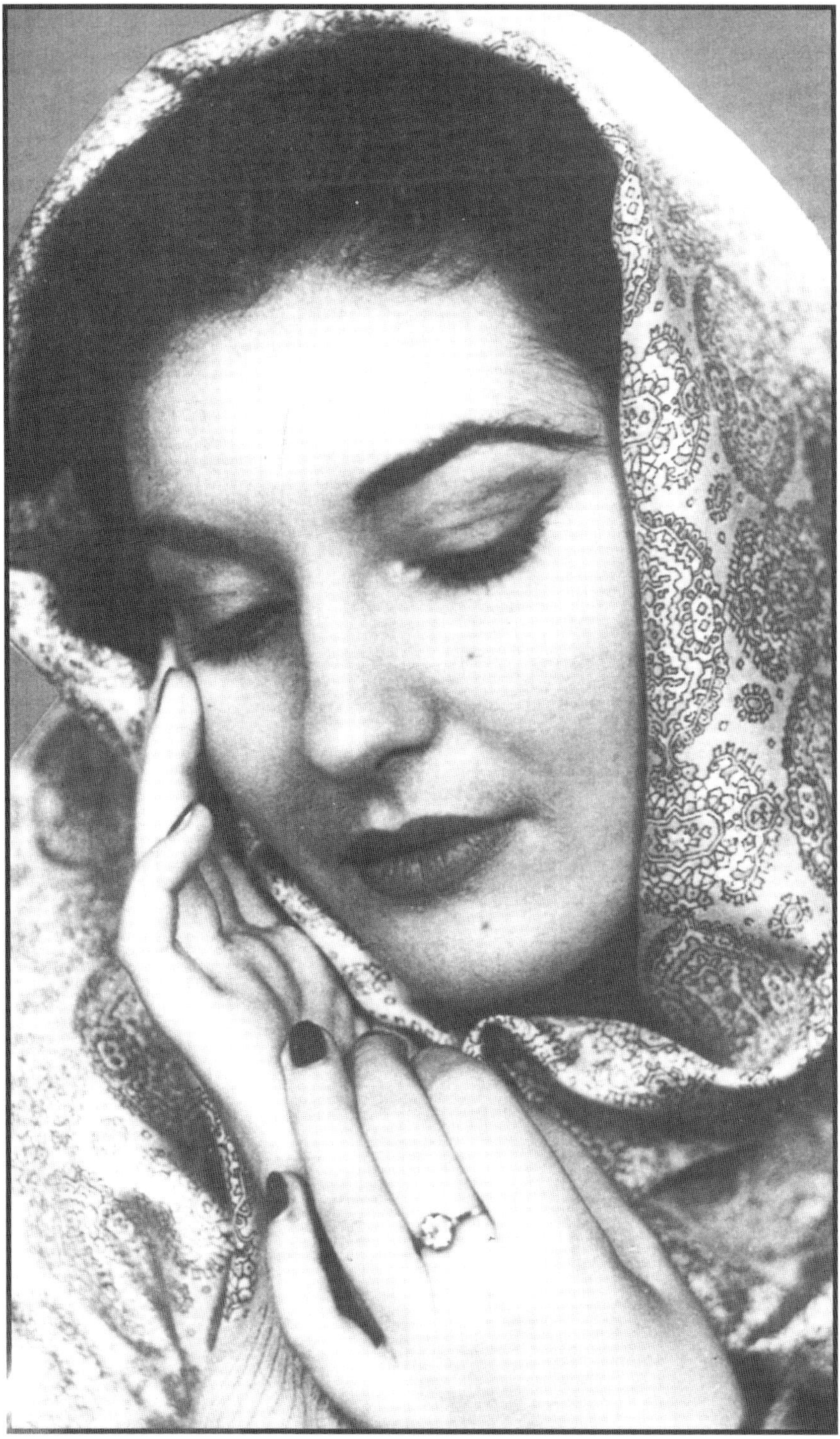

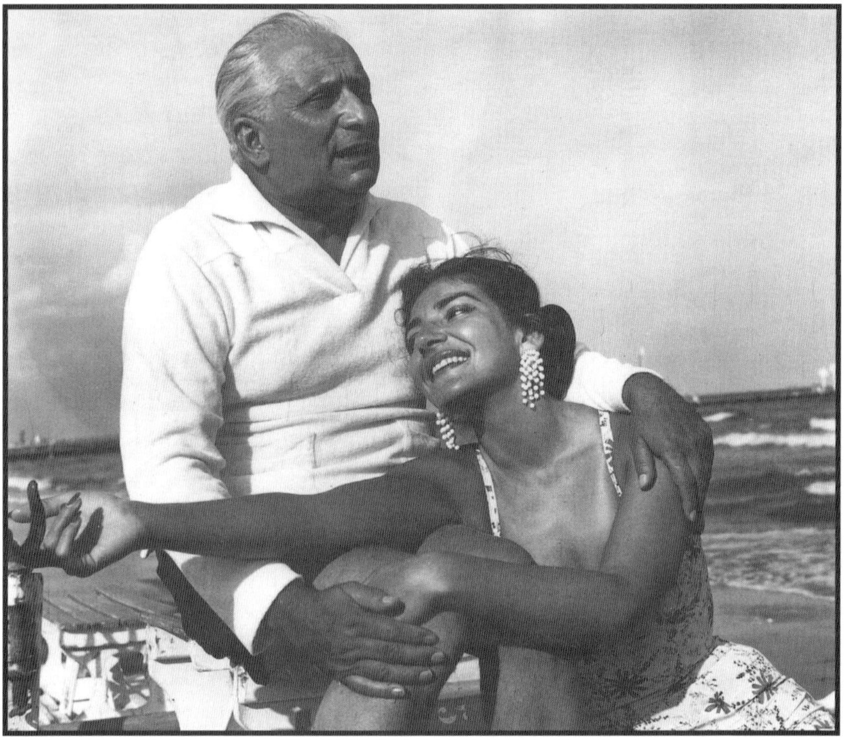

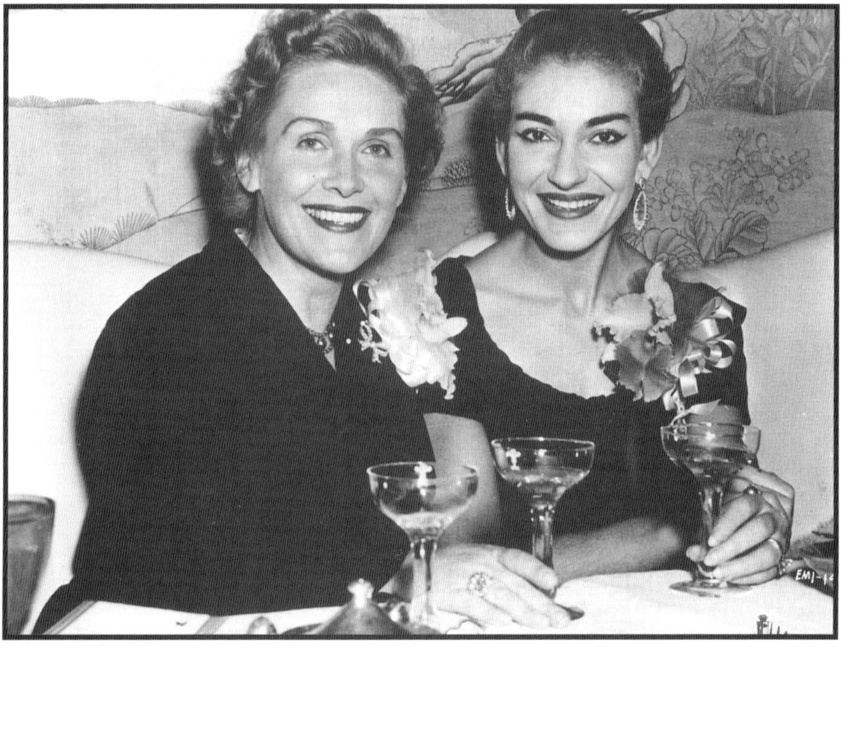

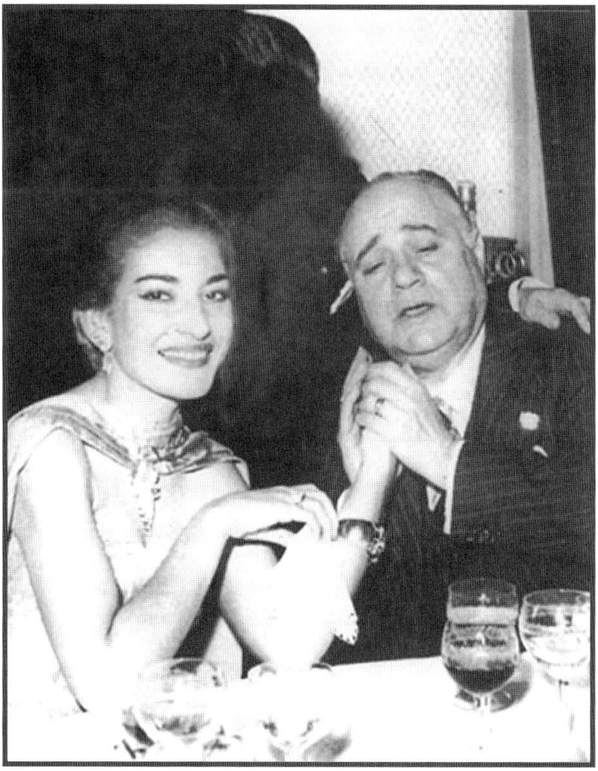

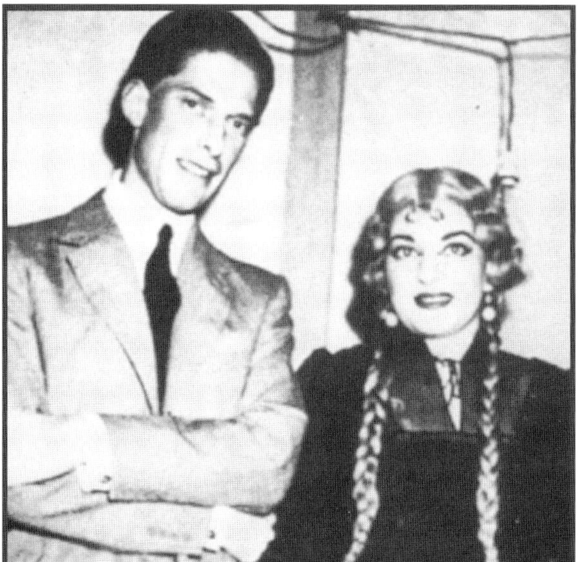

Anna Bolena - Scala di Milano 1957

the myth like very few other people: not the fêted singer, adored and acclaimed by her fans as the Voice of the century, but Maria Kalogeropoulos Meneghini.

In 1957, the preceding winter, I had started my career as a roving reporter with an article entitled "The Tebaldi-Callas wars." It was the moment of their historic rivalry that the Italians followed keenly more than anything else, more than the epic battle between the cyclists Bartoli and Coppi and the no less fierce rivalry between Sofia Loren and Gina Lollobrigida. I did not know Callas or Tebaldi personally and could not take sides with either of them. While I was collecting information for my article Callas had been described in less than glowing colors: no wonder we called her the Tigress while Tebaldi was always described as an Angel.

In the *Time* interview Maria had described Tebaldi as "A woman without a spine" and Renata had replied with a letter to the editor saying, "I have something that Callas does not have: a heart."

I had read in the American newspapers that on receiving a letter from her mother and her sister asking for financial help Callas had replied writing, *If you can't make do, throw yourselves out of the window!*

My article on the battle between the two golden voices of La Scala made my life hell. I received huge numbers of telephone calls, some praising but mostly abusive. Both the Callas and the Tebaldi camps attacked me, and some, particularly the Callasians, made threats.

Maria, on the other hand, was most kind about the whole event almost as though she had never heard of the article or me. We started our work together in an atmosphere of harmony and the result was the chronicle that tells of Callas' early years and ends just before the artist's cruise on the yacht of Aristotle Onassis: a cruise that, as we know, forever marked the life of the diva.

In 1957 the tape-recorder was not yet in common use and I would have to take notes by hand. I worked for several months several times per week till late at night. The ritual was always the same: Callas and I would work in a salon of the villa and after a few minutes of chatting we would start work, with me asking the questions and Callas answering, often rising from her chair and declaiming as though she was acting out a role. Even though he wanted to be there, I had banned Meneghini from attending; his being there would certainly have ruined the confidential ambiance that we had managed to create. He had no intention of leaving us alone and would walk about outside the door and try his best to listen in on the conversation. Every time we spoke about him, Maria would only use the phrase, "my husband." "Why don't you use his name?" I would ask: She, with beguiling innocence would answer in the soft Veronese accent she had learned from him, "But he's called Titta . . ." Clearly this diminutive seemed too funny for a diva.

I managed to persuade her that there was nothing to worry about and at that point she launched into praising him, chatting about their first shy meetings in Verona just after she had arrived from America onboard the "Stockholm" and virtually penniless with only her clothes and one pair of shoes to her name; the romantic weekend in Venice with Meneghini and Rossi Lemeni and his taking care of her when she was ill, unfortunately a frequent occurrence. At this point I jumped up, moved close to her and asked: "Why did you marry him?" She leaned over to me and in a whisper answered, "Who would have known that I was to become Callas?"

This episode proves that there is no doubt about Maria Kalogeropoulos and her amazing innate ability to split her personality without even being aware. Maria Kalogeropoulos and the Diva Callas had very little in common. During the war years in Athens the family's first concern was getting enough to eat leaving very little time for Maria to study. Her favorite reading matter was the ladies periodical, no longer in print, *Le vostre novelle* (Your stories) and every Thursday she would remind her maid with great anticipation, "Quick, run to the newsstand today, *Le vostre novelle* comes out . . ." Titta Meneghini told me that when one night he woke up to find Maria absent, he went downstairs and searched each room for her finally finding her on her knees sobbing dreadfully; on the floor next to her, the open score of *Madam Butterfly*. Maria had never read the story and the tragic end to Butterfly's story had distressed her terribly. On stage these soap opera characters became part of her art becoming magnificent heroines destined for immortality. I remember a *Medea* at La Scala. It was so perfect that I held my breath not wanting to break the spell of that incredible magic.

When she was Mrs. Meneghini, her life was divided between rehearsals and performances at Scala, the beautician, the dressmaker and the familiarity of her home. Only on the odd occasion when she could not refuse invitations would she go to a party or a premiere, but confessing to me, her favorite activity was occasionally to go shopping, her favorite store being *Rinascente*. She also aspired to acting in films. Maria told me, "You see, Anita, from the waist up, I'm quite photogenic and as far as my eyes, well, after all, they are undeniably beautiful."

After all: that is, she was so short sighted that on stage she could not even see the prompt box. To steer clear of disasters, directors would draw thick white lines on the stage that she could use as guidelines. Maria sang as though wrapped in a thick fog: any noise, even the far-off ringing of a bell would make her uneasy. She explained to me; "Yes, it's true I am oversensitive: when I'm concentrating I hate to be distracted by anything but I don't understand why others don't forgive me. If I wasn't like this I wouldn't be Callas."

Carrying on with the story of her life, she would often say: "I have got the hand of God on my head!" declaring herself like most Greeks, a fatalist. Nonetheless, even in her most desolate moments, she would make plans for the future. Reflecting on her circumstances she said, "Titta is twenty-eight years older than me and it's quite probable that I will be a widow."

The thought of being alone terrified her and she would scrutinize the list of possible replacements, some of whom I knew, married and with children. This was not an important obstacle to Maria. She had no fear of remorse; if she wanted something, it had to be hers and fast. In her choices and decisions she was clear and extreme. She was also aggressive, impulsive and like a force of nature. When, for example, during an important dinner she was unable to avoid making some blunder or statement void of any diplomacy, Meneghini, trying to stop her, would tap her leg with the point of his shoe. In a loud voice she would ask, "Titta, what are you doing? Why are you kicking me under the table?" While Meneghini was telling me this story, Maria watched us puzzled: She did not understand why we found it so amusing…

One evening, at the high point of the Callas-Tebaldi wars, after a performance at La Scala there was an inexplicable "Mystery" during the applause, Maria had bent down to pick up a bouquet thrown by a fan in the gallery. She brought it to her lips to kiss it, oblivious, owing to her shortsightedness did not see that it was not a bouquet of jasmine or gardenias but a bunch of vulgar and common turnips. "Who could have been the originator of so stupid an act?" the press asked. At once the Callas camp pointed a finger at the Tebaldians, who in this case were innocent: the deus ex machine was later proved to be an ex-teacher of Callas, an American whose name I do not recollect.

Finding herself in pecuniary difficulties she had come to Italy hopeful that Maria would help her out and solve her problems. She would wait outside the stage door in Via Filodrammatici and offer Maria a rose and ask for help. Maria would always ignore her and to make things worse on one occasion, opened her wide mouth and screamed, "I don't want to see you! If it had been up to you, no one would have ever heard of me. If I hadn't stopped my lessons with you in time you would have ruined my voice. Forever!" On the other hand, when Teodoro Celli, the critic from the weekly *Oggi* and I tried to put an end to the Callas-Tebaldi wars she was charming and appreciative. Together we had planned everything; the only thing missing was Renata's consent. One night, like conspirators, we crossed the park in Milan to get to the place where Renata was singing a concert. She received us courteously and listened to what we had to say, finally, looking at us with sadness and pride said, "I can't: my mother would turn in her grave." When Maria heard of our unsuccessful mission she smiled and said sighing, "I'm sorry, I was looking forward to it." Later Bing, the head of the Metropolitan persuaded the two to embrace in front of reporters and photographers in New York.

After Callas' society affair with Onassis their careers and paths never crossed again. As far as feminine charms were concerned Maria Kalogeropoulos had very few. Delicate health, thick ankles, obesity, and a marriage of convenience, "If only you knew how hard it was to get Meneghini to marry me," she told me. Her one true love Onassis, sordidly and publicly betrayed her; and finally the man who according to her plans was to be her companion, Giuseppe Di Stefano had, only one year before her death, refused to leave his wife for her.

Callas on the other hand had everything, a swift career, incredible triumphs and incredible contracts, including a film with Pasolini. She was the voice of the century the insuperable

Queen of singing. Yet the singer and the woman were by far too different to be able to understand each other and get along. When Maria died at only fifty-three, I went to Hamburg to interview Pippo Di Stefano who at the time was rehearsing *Zarevic,* an operetta by Lehar. Crying, he told me that he hadn't seen Maria since he had refused to give into her demands: "If you don't divorce your wife it's over between us." "We were not on the best of terms," he added with bitterness. "Maybe I should have stayed near her, somehow save our friendship. Music is what we had in common. I understood the greatness of Callas only after discovering the secrets of singing, it took me years and years." Then with a lump in his throat he said: "They tried to make Callas into an intellectual but she was like me; all instinct!" I was in total agreement with him but what I didn't know was that Maria was affected by glaucoma, which would increasingly have made her blind.

"Poor Maria," murmured Di Stefano, "she was always used by everybody especially Onassis. She loved him deeply and he used her, used her for public relations." "Why didn't he marry her?" I asked him.

Di Stefano replied: "Firstly, it's uncomfortable having a myth for a wife and secondly, because she was difficult; possessive, dominating and exasperating. She interfered and even tried to become involved in his oil tanker business. She treated him with condescension and looked down on him from the height of her fame. He, to get back at her accused her of being a simple performer, someone whose job it was to amuse the public. Onassis openly spoke of his disinterest in opera. They were worlds apart."

While I was writing Callas' memoirs Maria Kalogeropoulos-Meneghini still talked ironically about her alter ego. I saw her move, act, walk like an automaton but when she sat down in her own home in a dressing gown and slippers, she was simple and natural, a girl with incredible dreams. She must have suffered terribly during the second part of her life with Onassis. To keep up with the frenetic pace of his life she alternated tranquilizers with stimulants and consumed herself day by day. She protected her private life fiercely, and the day she found out from a television broadcast that her Ari was to marry Jacqueline Kennedy, she shut herself in her bedroom and wept in desperation.

When the tears were over, she made an appointment with Alexandre the society hairdresser to cancel all traces of sadness from her face and make her more beautiful than ever. She was expected at a gala dinner at Chez Maxim's and in front of all Parisian society she did not want to be Maria Kalogeropoulos but only "La Callas!"

SEVEN YEARS WITH MARIA

Pia Meneghini

I met Maria Callas on her arrival from America in June of 1947. She was shy, afraid and rather fat. She stayed at the Accademia Hotel in Verona where she had been sent by the Tenor Giovanni Zenatello who, together with a few of his relatives, was a co-owner of the hotel. The singer, even though having resided in New York for some years, was originally from Verona.

At that time there was not a soprano in Italy able to sing *La Gioconda*, the opera due to open the season of the Arena that year. Zenatello decided to give the role to Maria Callas after having heard her in New York at the suggestion of Nicola Rossi-Lemeni and Sergio Failloni, who was to conduct Ponchielli's masterwork.

Before meeting her I had heard a lot about her. The radio and the newspapers had already spoken about this ample young Greek woman who had arrived from America.

We knew that she had arrived on an ocean liner (America for us was so far away, almost a wonderland), and the fact that she had been chosen by Zenatello to sing in the Arena of Verona, which had only recommenced its opera season the previous year after the war years gave us cause to hope in something good . . . (She had just arrived in Verona and still spelled her name with a K, Kallas.) and I, like so many opera lovers, was very interested in seeing and hearing her in person.

It is part of history that Giovan Battista Meneghini was the first person to meet her in Verona and also to take an interest in her. I can add that immediately after him, I was the second. The encounter took place in Piazza Bra. She was introduced to Giovan Battista by Tullio Serafin and the directors of the Arena. Particularly after a sneaked trip to Venice an affectionate relationship developed quickly. She hung on his every word with devotion. I'm sure however that the valued counselor and friend had also been introduced to her as a very wealthy man. Maria certainly did not ignore this aspect: needy as she was, she did everything to chain him to her.

After about a month of studying alternately with Serafin and Cusinati, finally the opening night of *Gioconda* came. Unfortunately not under ideal conditions as Maria had sprained her ankle after a fall during rehearsals. It was the 2 August 1947. She sang under difficult and painful circumstances not being able to move much.

She later told me that she was in the habit of singing leaning on her right foot placed slightly in front of the left. This helped her with her voice, but the extreme pain did not permit her to do this. It is a known fact that the voice was certainly strong but technically still needed work.

Once the performances in the Arena were over there were no further offers of work. Titta (the name our family used for my brother) managed to get her a contract to sing *Tristan and Isolde* at the Fenice in Venice which was premiered there on the 30 December 1947.

Before accepting her, Serafin gave her an audition and insisted that she transfer to Rome to study the opera with him note by note. It was an intense fifteen days. Even though we had only known each other a short time she asked me to go with her. I accepted with enthusiasm. From the start of her glittering career right up to the first signs off her voice failing her (when also due to familial problems our relationship became less close), I was her friend, sister-in-law and confidante.

Maria was not an optimist. She needed constant encouragement and stimulation. She was extremely insecure and would often let herself get upset. She had a desperate need for comfort and company. This support she certainly found in my brother and me. We were a family and she would often say: "This is my whole world, thanks to you I am reborn; I appreciate it and don't want anything else."

Poor Maria, she was content with very little. It was her voice that gave us everything. Serafin too noticed how close we were and said often, "I can see that your presence is indispensable to Maria, I do not know what she would do without you." Such expressions of honor coming from so illustrious and sensitive a man I accepted with real devotion.

It was not always easy to be close to her. She always doubted her voice and was never content; the fear of failure depressed her. She always found fault with her voice and feared that others would notice too. She always expected bad notices and reviews. It was like a refrain, a lament that became an obsession during the long days of rehearsals awaiting the opening.

A year after her career had taken off so brilliantly, she invited her sister Jackie Kalogeropoulos, seven years her senior, to visit her in Verona. Physically she was very different from Callas: Jackie was tall and slender; she too dreamed of an artistic career but was not talented at all. She arrived with little luggage as had Maria the previous year and carrying a small cage containing a rather sad looking canary that she had not wanted to abandon. During her stay in Verona Jackie visited us regularly and we came to like her. On her departure she gave my son Piero the large cage she had bought in Verona for the canary and took it back in the smaller less cumbersome one she had arrived with. I never saw her again. Her relationship with Maria had deteriorated gradually. Her mother and sister who lived in Athens in difficult financial circumstances expected to receive some sort of help from her. But Callas, whenever I mentioned it to her would answer: "For what they did for me, I have no obligation to help them."

After the first successes in Venice the Italian theaters started to call and the performances started to overlap each other. The Politeama of Trieste asked her to do several performances of *Forza del Destino* in April 1948. Maria asked my mother Giuseppina Meneghini to accompany us to the performance.

At that time, to travel to Trieste one had to have valid travel documents. "Signora," they said, "you cannot pass, as your identity card has expired." It was just like the era of Mussolini. Both Maria's and my brother's passports had expired two days previously. I was the only person in the group with valid documents. The police said to me, "Only you can pass." "The problem," I said smiling, "is that I cannot replace the lady sitting in the rear of the car, she is the one who has to sing today in Trieste." After a few minutes a car with a Verona number plate approached and a gentleman got out with his document ready to be inspected. He recognized us immediately and said, "What are you doing here?" It was Engineer Aurelio Todeschini from Zevio, our neighbor.

Fortunately he had a magazine with him that contained an article about Maria and managed to convince the policemen of her identity. We managed to get to the theater and the performance went on without further mishap. For Callas, once an opera had been performed, getting ready without preamble was no problem. She only needed the time to do light make-up; her eyes only, she never used foundation as it hardened her face. I would fasten her costume and she was ready for the stage. I must say that it was always a pleasure watching her do her make-up. She would change her expression with small movements. She always did it herself, fast and at the same time with great calm. She used very little lipstick and would transform her face with great ease. Her make-up bag was always full of creams, oils and unguents that she never used. Very little perfume and always the best brands, just right for each occasion and time of the day. Regarding her eyes, it is well known the Maria was near-sighted but I never heard her complain of this fact.

On stage she couldn't see the conductor but never missed an entry. She hardly ever wore contact lenses as she found them irritating. Nonetheless her eyes were always brilliant and vivacious: she knew how to express anger, happiness, irritability and joy.

Before La Scala, the Teatro Comunale in Florence played an important part in her career with the ground-breaking performances of various operas thanks to the genius and intuition of Francesco Siciliani who convinced Parise Votto to call Callas to perform her first *Norma*. It was November 30, 1948, and I remember at the end of the performance Serafin rushed into her dressing room and without holding back the tears held her hand for a long time and limited his words to: "Maria, you're great."

Even though Maria was surrounded by people who understood her talent she was still doubtful. "Pia," she would say to me, "you never know what tricks the voice might play: we cannot permit ourselves to rest on our laurels." Enormous preoccupations, her sense of responsibility and self-criticism certainly did not make life easy for her. This was how she started to take the advice of various doctors including my husband Dr. Gianni Cazzarolli, who became her personal physician, and Professor Coppo of the University of Modena who owned a beautiful villa in the hills surrounding Verona. When, during the performances of *Norma* in Florence, Maria was incapacitated by an attack of appendicitis. Dr. Cazzarolli immediately arrived from Verona. As soon as Maria saw him she exclaimed, "Now I will go on stage." It was the final performance and all went well. Maria was operated on immediately afterwards with success. She regained her serenity and her voice improved.

At the beginning of 1949 she returned to the Fenice in Venice to perform *Walkyrie* super-prepared according to Serafin. Everything went well: she was acclaimed by the public and the reviews were excellent. A few days later the second opera due to be performed was *I Puritani* with the coloratura soprano Margherita Carosio. Unfortunately a sudden lung hemorrhage prohibited her from performing. Frequent recurrences unfortunately brought to an end a splendid career.

Serafin, who was conducting both operas, was very worried. After his wife, a noted dramatic soprano, had advised him, he decided to try Maria in the role. The first thing he did was go through the mad scene. Satisfied he said, "That's it. We'll do the opera and you will be Elvira. Over the next few days right up to the first night you must work hard day and night." And so it was. Maria alternated her performances of *Walkyrie* with rehearsals of *Puritani* becoming in the process the ideal interpreter of Bellini's masterpiece.

On the opening night, Carosio's name was covered with strips of paper and Maria's name substituted. The great to-do made Carosio's fans jealous and we were advised by the directors of the theater to pay the claque. Maria was furious and refused: "I don't give a fig for their whistles unless I warrant them." My brother also refused.

It was my turn and they convinced me to quietly pay out a tidy sum, a secret I have kept till now. It was the only time we ever did this for Maria, a disgusting habit that is still all too frequent in the theater. That evening the theater was filled with people who had come from Milan and Rome to hear the Phenomenon Callas. The enthusiasm was unanimous.

Only Maria, still incredulous, said, "Yes, it went well but I've still got a lot of studying to do."

Maria was always generous to me. After her first successes she decided to renew her wardrobe and had some fur coats sent from America. She had sent my measurements along with hers, so I received a beaver coat and a fabulous white mink jacket cut to perfection and greatly admired by all at various gala evenings in Rome. At that time only Wanda Osiris had a white mink coat. Maria said, "I'm very happy with these purchases and that you are satisfied; my little sister-in-law must always be perfect at all times of the day with or without me."

And so we come to the wedding. Maria wanted my brother, who had been instrumental in her successes, all for herself. She dreamed of changing her name to Maria Callas Meneghini or rather Maria Meneghini Callas. My brother certainly was devoted to her but seemed uninterested in taking that final step. In seeing him reticent, Maria asked for my help and my complicity. "If Battista doesn't marry me," the daily refrain, "I'll just return to America and follow my own destiny." There were also religious obstacles to overcome, she being Greek Orthodox and my brother a Catholic. Maria's difficult character was certainly no help either in Battista making up his mind. She was irascible, capricious and obstinate. She wanted everything and immediately. He did feel a genuine affection for her and in a way considered himself her Pygmalion, her guardian angel, but was not in love with her.

In order to be with her all the time, he would have to abandon the direction of the family business and to create some sort of an alibi, he brought his brothers into the affair, and they really had nothing to do with it. The truth of the matter was that it was her voice that had cast a spell on him: He avoided the woman to discover the artist. The woman, Maria, was decidedly willful. She would repeat to me: "I want Battista for myself and I don't care about the difference in age. Even if I was born in 1923 and he in 1895, I look older than I am."

One Friday evening I had organized a dinner at the home of Engineer Mario Orlandi with a menu of polenta and baccala, a favorite of Maria's. Lying on a *dormeuse* she refused to come to the table. "Pia," she said, "can't you see the state I'm in? I can't go on."

I returned to the dining room and said to my brother, "Maria is in a bad way. Either you decide yes or leave her free." He whispered a very weak "yes" and I ran to Maria to tell her. She insisted on hearing it from his own lips. Once her crying and palpitations had stopped she came to the table, ate greedily and laughed and made toasts. She had won her battle. After three days of pressure from my brother, the Verona Curia decided that they would approve the marriage between a Catholic and a Greek Orthodox.

The wedding took place on April 29, 1949, at five in the afternoon in the sacristy of the Church of the Fillipini in Verona. The witnesses were my husband for Battista and Engineer Orlandi for Maria. I was unable to attend the service as I had been charged with organizing the wedding dinner at my home. I remember the menu: antipasto of caviar, a cheese *flou*, consomme, roast guinea-fowl, red radicchio and wedding cake. For the floral decorations I used my florist Ghedini, the best in the city. Red roses and an enormous bouquet of forget-me-nots. The table was covered with a white organza tablecloth and the service was antique silver and crystal goblets.

The next day Maria left alone for a tour of Argentina. On her return she found that she had a new home in Stradone San Fermo number 21, entirely decorated by me: Antique furniture which was simple and with fine workmanship. In the bedroom there were two tables by Maggiolini with oval mirrors and frames by Brustolon, a prie-dieu and a Madonna by Frolli holding a beautiful curly haired baby Jesus. The entrance hall ended in a long corridor ending with a niche. A hidden light illuminated a Madonna attributed to Titian hung above a beautiful wooden settle. I still jealously guard a beautiful Madonna of Guadalupe set in a fine gold medal that Maria bought in Argentina and gave to me on her return in thanks for all I had done for her.

The Comunale in Florence offered Maria the Stradella oratorio *San Giovanni Battista* to be performed in the church of San Pietro in Perugia. Before accepting she went to Torri del Benaco to visit Serafin who was there with Cusinati to seek their advice. After a week of study we went to Perugia. The atmosphere of these places gave her a great sense of peace and calm. She was particularly struck with Assisi. One afternoon returning from a relaxing walk we found a group of students waiting for us in the foyer of the Hotel Brufani where we were staying. Calmly and with grace Maria allowed them a brief conversation. They all had questions and she was most expansive in her replies and advice. One beautiful Sunday in September 1949 the oratorio was performed. At the end of the first part, during the interval, Maria suggested that we visit the beautiful church. Our tour was interrupted when we were asked to return to the sacristy. The first part had been recorded and they wanted to surprise her. After listening briefly Maria exclaimed, "This woman sings wonderfully, she has a beautiful voice." "But no! Don't you recognize it, it's you singing," they said.

Maria burst into tears. She was not used to hearing her own voice and couldn't believe that that sound came from her own throat. I learned later that she only had one recording of her own voice, a recording of "O mio bambino caro" from Puccini's

Gianni Schicchi that she had made when she was twelve or thirteen years old and guarded jealously.

In January of 1950 Maria was in Venice to perform *Norma* conducted by Antonino Votto. I arrived to find her in bed, completely hoarse. She received me with a wan smile, unable to utter a single word. The room was tiny and overheated. I told her that she couldn't possibly stay in that room with that suffocating heat and dry air. I ordered the chambermaid to bring wet cloths and large sponges that I then placed on the radiators. Maria was worried about that evening's performance and was afraid she would not be able to sing. Maria asked me to fetch some honey and anything that might be able to give her back her voice. I went to a nearby pharmacy and spent the rest of the afternoon trying everything from infusions to inhalations old and tried remedies.

At six o'clock, not seeing any improvement, she asked me to inform Votto. I started towards the stairs where I found him ready to leave for the theatre already in tails, black cloak and white scarf. When I told him that Maria had lost her voice he was stunned. He thought it was a whim and not a real illness. I asked him to verify for himself and he followed me to Maria's room. He insisted that she get dressed and go to the theater where he tried in vain to get her to sing. Not a single sound would come out of her mouth and the performance was postponed by two days.

Undoubtedly, La Scala is the dream of all singers. The theater that was to become her home at first rejected her. The artistic director Mario Labroca, after hearing her in 1947, had told my brother that he would save time and money by sending her back to America. Fortunately Tullio Serafin supported her and repeatedly told her, "Maria, don't worry, your defects will become your assets and you will drive the public wild." Soon the doors of La Scala were opened to her. Antonio Ghiringhelli contracted her for performances of operas that would go down in history. Maria was now able to demonstrate her great art and versatility in a vast repertoire.

Maria's first opera at La Scala was *Aida* in April 1950. Immediately afterwards she was called to San Carlo in Naples for the same opera. She did not ask me to go with her and so I decided to do a few things around the house that I'd been putting off till the moment arose. However, the same day that she arrived in Naples my brother called me and begged me to leave immediately as she wanted me there as soon as possible. I arrived before evening and found Maria in bed crying. When I asked her the reason for her crying she said, "The maestro doesn't like my first and second act costume." I reassured her saying that I was sure he would accept it in the end. The costume was a simple yellow tunic with a twenty centimeter wide diagonal multicolored sash crossing her breast and skirt. Probably the real problem was the long split up the side that would have exposed Maria's ample thigh. Serafin was rather attentive to these sort of details. Thanks to the dark make-up and a modification to the opening on the side, to Serafin it seemed a new and beautiful costume. On the opening night Maria was magnificent. I knocked on the Maestro's door and asked him to inspect Maria. Seeing his Aida, he limited himself to one word pronounced in his deep voice, "Bella." The theater was full, so full that the doors had to be left open and crowds of people remained standing for the entire performance.

At the end of the opera there was the problem of removing the make-up. I had a look in Maria's bathroom. Horror! The bath, the floor, everything was a sticky black mess. I don't know how many of the dancers had used it at the end of the triumphal scene to remove their make-up. There was no more hot water and the head of the theater Di Costanzo didn't know what to do and was fearful of Maria's reaction. I ran back to her and told her that her back had a bad skin irritation and that taking a bath right then would be harmful. "I can't leave like this," she said. I said I would take care of everything and cleaned her perfectly with some soft paper tissues that I had with me, convincing her to wait till her arrival in the hotel before taking a bath. For years Di Costanzo thanked me for avoiding a terrible scene.

When not performing Maria loved going to the theater and enjoyed comedies and shows, favoring Cervi and Pagnani. We went often and would meet up with them in their dressing rooms and later go out to dinner, frequently staying out till four in the morning. Normally the following day Maria would stay in bed till two o'clock due to her low blood pressure. Serafin followed all these goings on. He would invite me to lunch with him but I always refused knowing that Maria needed me. "You make too many sacrifices," he would say, "but I know how much she needs you." In spite of his apparent calm, Serafin would need to change his shirt between acts and as his wife did not always accompany him he had an elderly lady in his service to help him.

My brother would usually arrive by whatever fast means available just before the start of the performance. I felt really sorry for him: he would remain agitated for hours after the end of the opera and could never enjoy the warmth of the applause.

One day Maria said, "Pia, I want to give you a photo of me, a beautiful portrait." I thanked her adding that I did not want a picture of her in costume but a photo of her as she really was, showing her hair and her hands, both of which were beautiful She had lovely long fingers that were so expressive in movement. She did her own nails and they were always perfect. She wore her dark hair which had titian high-lights in a thick braid that she wound around her head framing her beautiful face. It was the loveliest gift I had ever received and is still in pride of place in my salon. She wrote: "To my dear Pia, with sincere affection."

On March 19, 1952, we celebrated the wedding of my son Angelo to Cecilia Stoppa. Maria, who was fond of us, always participated in family celebrations with great joy. When the word got out that she would be there, an enormous crowd filled the church of San Giovanni Fuori le Mura, the piazza and the nearby streets. The groom and I had to get to the church on foot. What unforgettable memories! The four corners of the altarpiece were covered with white carnations while the pew of the wedding party was hung with lily of the valley brought directly from the green-houses outside Florence. The wedding dinner was served by Harry's Bar of Venice and overseen by Cipriani himself.

In March of 1953 I saw Giuseppe Di Stefano for the first time. We were at the Carlo Felice theater in Genova where Maria was singing *Lucia di Lammermoor*. One Sunday morning, the new tenor, at least he was to me, came up to me and asked: "I don't have any money for lunch, do you think Maria could lend me thirty thousand lire?" I could have lent the money myself but instead turned to Maria and let her reply. He had the sort of face that immediately inspires one with confidence and *simpatia*. Maria consented and at the end of the first act of the performance, the magnificent Pippo paid his debt. Di Stefano was one of the most highly regarded tenors by Maria, not only for his voice but his qualities as a human being. Immediately they enjoyed a deep and sincere affection.

For the coronation of Queen Elizabeth II, Covent Garden in London had invited Maria and other illustrious artists to perform. The operas chosen were *Aida*, *Norma* and *Trovatore*. Among the cast were the bass Giulio Neri and the new rising star, the mezzo Giulietta Simionato. The gala evening was to be *Aida* but the Queen insisted on an English opera and so we heard *Gloriana*. What a disaster! The only thing worth remembering, was seeing the Royal Box with the all the dignitaries. I was particularly struck by the Queen's dress and jewels. I was wearing my white mink coat while Maria was wearing a long dress with a blue cloak. While staying at the Savoy I met a number of artists and celebrities who had arrived from all over the world to take part in the month long festivities. The city was filled with flowers, imported for the events. We could only travel in special taxis and Maria always had one at her disposal. I immediately got into the good graces of the Italian Ambassador's wife for having made favorable comments about some splendid tapestries I'd seen in the dining room. "They are the only works of note in the whole embassy," she said, "but none of the Italian guests even noticed them." During our stay in London we also met Lord Harewood, a cousin of the Queen and a great opera lover. Every year he would come to Verona and see the operas in the Arena incognito. The Duke of Kent's family was also at the Savoy. Also a Maharajah with his wife and eight concubines. How could I forget Maurice Chevalier, who had arrived from America for his one performance. One morning in a large department store I recognized Maria Pia di Savoia, her eyes and face so similar to those of her father. "I'm Italian," I said. Offering her hand she replied, "Maria Pia." I asked her for news of her father and she said he was well. I said that I was with my sister-in-law and presented Maria who was standing nearby. She recognized her immediately and exclaimed, "Norma." She had been present at the performance. We moved closer to Maria and had a very pleasant conversation.

All the operas performed at Covent Garden were a great success. Maria reigned as a Queen on the stage. In the romantic scenes requiring her to be close to the tenor she always preferred to keep a certain distance and always measured the idyllic love scenes with class. During a rehearsal in London she interrupted a duet and walked off-stage. The tenor had embraced her and did not keep his distance respecting the pact made with her beforehand. She did not return to the theater that day. The tenor sent her a huge bouquet of flowers and, pacified, she returned to do the performance.

I never tired of this fabulous period. The only thing I missed in London was our blue sky.

I asked one of the maids at the Savoy, "Don't you ever see a clear sky here with sunshine?" She answered, "When there is I'll call you." One day she rushed up to me and said, "Come outside, Madam," all excited. I followed her and saw the sky partially cleared: For the English a beautiful day. Maria asked me where I'd been and when I told her she burst out laughing. Life with Callas was splendid. My brother however never could enjoy these extraordinary aspects of her life. The more splendid the occasion, the more nervous he became. He took it out on conductors (only Serafin reassured him), agents, Maria's colleagues and the servants. The press did not always put things the way he'd have liked. Even one little mistake like her name not being given enough prominence would be the end of the world. Maria did not particularly care.

Giulietta Simionato had also been praised highly for her Adalgisa in *Norma* and Amneris in *Aida*. Maria was worried that in *Trovatore* Azucena would shine more brilliantly than Leonora. Certainly the two artists were friends but a bit of rivalry in the theater is always present. Fortunately, things went well and Giulietta had her triumph in the second act, and Maria triumphed in the last act and so they celebrated the triumph together. Outside the theater Maria was surrounded by her admirers and we were escorted all the way back to the Savoy.

In 1953 Maria decided to change her look totally and lose 35 kilos in a few months. Her diet was the subject of a thousand suppositions. After having seen the film *Roman Holiday* with Audrey Hepburn, Maria was obsessed with the idea of looking like her. Looking at the photos of her in that period one can see that once she had achieved the figure of a model she copied and imitated her right down to her hairstyle. I am the only person who really knows the secret of Maria's remarkable transformation. She asked me to promise never to tell anyone about it and used the romantic story of the tape-worm washed down with champagne as a cover. In truth it was even more horrible. Against the advice of Titta and my husband, her personal physician, she underwent a dangerous treatment from a group of Swiss doctors. She was administered large doses of dry thyroid extract and hormones with the aim of speeding up her metabolism eliminating excess fat in a brief time. Also, impatient with the results and wanting to speed things up further, she had iodine applied directly into the thyroid. This was a shock treatment that gave her an enviable figure but it permanently altered her metabolism and her nervous system also damaging her voice. Diets such as these are very dangerous for the cardio-vascular system and have to be undertaken with great care; the patient is putting his life in serious danger. Maria disappeared totally from Verona (she had already decided to move to Milan with my brother), and put herself into the care of a Milanese doctor and two Swiss doctors. As far as the story of the tape-worm, Maria did have an infection for a period without knowing about it. She was particularly fond of cured and preserved meat and by eating salami she was infected by this annoying parasite.

Early one morning in September 1953, I received a call from Maria telling me that she was not feeling well and had spent the night unable to sleep and when she did she had nightmares. She wanted to spend time away from the family and the only place nearby that was quiet enough was the Lido of Venice. She had never had a sea-side holiday since her arrival in Italy and now, thanks to her diet she was much slimmer and could wear a bathing costume without embarrassment. "Come with me," she said. Naturally I accepted immediately. One of my passions is Venice, the lagoon and the sea. We stayed at the Hotel des Bains spending carefree days on the beach and dining at the Taverna La Fenice or the Colombo restaurant. An unforgettable holiday!

The following December we were in Milan for the performances of *Medea* with Bernstein conducting. During one of the free days during rehearsals, Maria suggested that we visit the famous dress maker De Hidalgo at his atelier, "He is the brother of my teacher Elvira De Hidalgo," she said. Maria always had fond memories of her teacher who had not only noticed her potential but had encouraged her in her most unhappy moments in Greece.

De Hidalgo's brother had also taken an interest in Maria and her meteoric rise to fame and, even though she was still quite heavy, he tried to discourage her from losing any more weight fearing that she would damage her voice.

One evening in 1954, the last we were to spend together, Maria had just arrived from Milan. She was wearing a knitted gray suit. I said to her, "You are 1.73m tall and have achieved an enviable 70 kgs, don't lose any more weight, it could affect your voice." She replied that she wanted to lose five or six more. She was already beautiful. Before taking leave she prepared me a cold drink. Neither of us had ever taken alcoholic drinks and with her diet she had also given up pastries and sweets. At two o'clock that morning my daughter-in-law gave birth prematurely to a beautiful baby boy.

It was a very difficult delivery, costing her two months of being in a life and death situation. I no longer had the strength to run to Maria and follow her around as I had so lovingly done for seven years. She called me on the phone and said: "Why don't you come to me, why are you sacrificing yourself for that woman?" At her insistence I answered that she could not understand and that I would never treat my family as she had treated her mother and sister. She was terribly offended! These words caused the end of our friendship. I have often over the years regretted those words. Perhaps if I had been closer to her she would not have descended into the abyss that gradually consumed her.

I did, however follow her career from a distance. Maria continued her drastic diet without caring about the consequences it would have on that voice that she, years before, had told me was so subject to playing tricks on her.

One of the first times she had a problem was in Bergamo. It was a small incident during the first act of *Lucia di Lammermoor*: She opened her mouth and nothing came out for an instant. I was in the theater and felt a great sense of pain for her. Was this the beginning of the end? I did not want to accept the idea. During the interval I left the theater for a cup of coffee. I needed one. I heard the cashier of the cafe say in a loud voice, "Callas missed a note, a big one." It was not a big "Stecca" but certainly the voice disappeared for an instant.

The second time I noticed with sadness that her voice was in decline was in Rome where she was to sing *Norma* in January of 1958. I was in Cortina at the Hotel Savoia and at nine o'clock I turned on the radio as they were broadcasting it live from the theater in Rome. The president of Italy, Gronchi, was present. I awaited her entry with trepidation and as soon as she started to sing I realized something was wrong. Alongside the applause there were a few whistles and invectives. Maria decided to not finish the performance, her way of protesting against a public that had betrayed her. My brother was extremely on edge and accused everyone around him of being the guilty party. Once the performance had been cancelled, President Gronchi, who had arranged to be fetched at midnight by his driver had to be taken home in an ordinary police patrol car. The next morning I ordered all the newspapers to be brought to my room. Front page news was the disaster at the Rome Opera.

Maria sang other operas but the power and edge of her voice was only a memory. Finally after having separated from my brother, no longer Titta but Commendatore Meneghini, Onassis dead, she did a final tour with Di Stefano. It was acclaimed thanks to her myth, certainly not for the voice that in the past had earned her the title of Diva.

At her height, I counted up to twenty-five people in a box. With her interpretations and her way of wearing costumes, with her tenacity and dramatic flair, she had taken the public to new heights of delirium. I am reminded of many anecdotes and memories. The wonderful moments spent with Maria. The knowledge that I had taken part in so many of her triumphs. My husband, a cultured and intelligent man had become very fond of his illustrious patient and let me spend a great deal of time to taking care of Maria. I managed to balance my obligations to my family and to her without anyone feeling left out.

One of the people I had become close to was Elena Rakowska, Maestro Serafin's wife. I would often meet her in Rome. We had seen Maria's first operas in Rome together. Her first *Norma*, her first *Traviata*, her *Turco in Italia* at the Eliseo conducted by Gavazzeni. Rakowska told me that she had fond memories of Verona, having sung *Francesca da Rimini* at the Teatro Filarmonico. I remember going to the performance with my brother. The title had made me curious and I asked Battista to take me. He was amazed at my proposal and said that little girls in short socks were not allowed in, only ladies elegantly dressed. "I'll be well-dressed," I answered. I prepared myself for my "debut" at the theater: a skirt and a blouse embroidered with silver and gold thread; black patent leather shoes with a low heel; Battista was so moved by my enthusiasm that he immediately bought two tickets in the stalls. From that moment I showed a sincere interest and predisposition towards music. I never would have imagined that I was to become so close to Maria Callas.

Madam Serafin was always highly appreciative of Maria's qualities and vocal method. Listening to *Casta Diva,* she once said to me: "If I was in her place waiting for the cabaletta, I'd have a fever of at least 40 degrees." She understood Maria even more than the maestro. Whenever we were her guests in Rome she would prepare her favorite Russian dishes for us.

Maria was a woman of enormous intelligence: she learned new operas and foreign languages with great ease, and was blessed with a remarkable sense of intuition that did not allow her to make mistakes. I often heard the great Maestros ask her, "How would you interpret this phrase?" Her answers were always fast, lucid and exact. She had a sad childhood, little family affection, separated parents and great poverty.

This did not allow her much in the way of choice; for her everything was plain "yes" or "no." This lack of diplomacy and her tortured sense of always needing approval caused her endless problems. Sometimes she could be sweet and generous. I remember a particular occasion when I asked her on the return journey from Florence to Verona where she had been singing *Lucia,* to make a detour and give a small concert for some students at Pavullo, a small town between Abetone and Modena. She agreed immediately. What a joy it was, the applause, the enthusiasm of the young public. "It is I who thank you," Maria said, quite moved. Other times she could be quite unpredictable. She had recently moved to Milan, still very much in love with her husband. They had taken along Matilde, an elderly maid. One morning quite suddenly, just before leaving the house she turned to her husband and said, "I'm going to La Scala for a rehearsal and when I return I no longer want to find Matilde here. You can take care of sending her wherever you like." Battista had no choice but to pack her bags and send her back to Verona without an explanation. With the public Maria seemed indifferent: she never put herself in the position of being dependent or subjugated.

In all her dealings with people, even those of importance, she expected to be treated and treated everyone as equal. "When I sing, all the labor is mine," she would say. But if you were to perform in an empty theater, no applause or praise from your admirers, what satisfaction would you feel?" This was a question that she was never able to answer.

She was a woman who could cause lightning to strike from a clear sky. I can't remember how many times my brother would repeat, "You have to be very careful how you behave around her. A mere trifle can turn the most idyllic situation into a disaster." He also would never have thought that his love for her would be destroyed. He believed he would have a tranquil old age. It was not to be.

I do not have any regrets for the years I dedicated to her. Rather, I am sad and embittered that it was I that sparked the breakdown in our friendship. If things had been otherwise, I often wonder how Maria's life might have been different. At this point I'd like to mention an unusual moment. One evening during a performance of *Turandot* in the Arena, both Callas and Tebaldi were in the house. During the interval along with my companion, the widow of Otorino Respighi, the two prima donnas chatted like old friends, remembering moments of their careers with great joy. Unfortunately that evening no photographers caught the moment. The press had always preferred to exaggerate the differences and difficulties between the two divas.

I have heard of ardent love letters from Maria to her husband Titta. I'm surprised. The dates do not always correspond with her absences at that time, added to which I never saw her put pen to paper. She would say: "When I need to say something to my husband I do it quickly on the phone." I never saw any of those letters that were published in the magazines. So as not to disappoint all the admirers that wrote to Maria asking for an autographed photo, often Titta would answer having first studied her signature and later her handwriting exactly. This is valid for numerous contracts too. I don't want to be spiteful but what if it was temptation that may have caused my brother to write those letters himself, the letters he would have desired to receive from Maria? In the beginning it was Maria who was the one in love and once the ugly duckling had been transformed, it was Titta who realized that it was he who could not live without her. The affair with Onassis nearly drove him mad. Then Callas was left when Onassis decided to marry Jacqueline Kennedy. Giovan Battista went to Paris several times, calling out her name under her windows. Maria refused to see him.

Under the weight of her premature vocal decline she had withdrawn into herself completely and not even the love she had for Di Stefano could give her the will to live.

Recorded by Bruno Tosi

THE YOUNG CALLAS

Bruno Tosi

If you serve art well, everything will come automatically: you will be great, you will have money, there will be fame. But the work is hard, in the beginning, during and afterwards.

But it is a privilege. I consider myself privileged because I have been able to bring truth from the soul and the mind, give it to the public, and have it accepted. Not everyone can do that. It is one of the greatest powers one can put at the service of one of the greatest arts: music.

These words, almost a précis of her career, by Maria Callas in March 1972, were spoken to students at the Juilliard School of Music in New York. The hall was filled for every lesson with illustrious colleagues, students and personalities from the world of the arts and culture, eager to listen to every word she said.

Master Class, the play by Terence McNally, has become an international success and after being performed by famous actresses in Los Angeles and New York, it has been done in London, Paris and Tokyo and has been a great success in Italy with the role of Callas being played by Rosella Falk.

Callas said these words at the final lesson just before taking her leave. She had remained in contact with Pasolini after her film of *Medea* and a deep and affectionate correspondence had developed. She said in a recent letter to him: *I think that my contact with these young people, lost in the dark, without belief, without example, will do me good and maybe be good for them too. At least I will try.* The young Callas many years before had suffered the same anguish, the same waiting. All she had gained had cost her dearly. She had often found herself "lost in the dark," in particular her interlude in New York, after the hard work in Athens and before her career took off in Verona and Venice. Three disheartening years were spent persistently trying to get work and be accepted in America. Only her strong willpower, ambition and her unshakeable faith allowed her to rise above the anxious moments when everything was collapsing around her. All this left her with a permanent sense of bitterness and mistrust.

The title of this book is *The Young Maria Callas,* but as far as is apparent or imaginable, she was never young. Even as a child she was deprived of the carefree times to play like other children could. Destiny had decreed, or rather her mother had decided; at little more than eight years old she was performing in talent contests on the radio to win prizes. This might on the one hand have been gratifying, but her being thrown into the limelight so soon must also have traumatized her. "There should be a law against this sort of thing." Callas's own words were spoken in a bitter interview whilst talking about her early years, "At the cost of going against families and ambitious mothers who in their fanaticism are speculating on their children. It is not right to deprive a child of its childhood, moreover, that particular unconditional love which becomes a precious memory in later years, something to look back on fondly forever." She also later said, "I felt forced: I only felt loved when I sang, and that is terrible."

It is a well-known fact that Angelia Kalogeropoulos favored her firstborn daughter Jackie, six years older than Maria. She was beautiful and had a good figure and, according to the family, had a better voice. This rivalry and the harshness of her mother would cause a whole host of complexes and frustrations. A story is told that to stop her crying, as a baby, her mother would put a pinch of pepper on her lips.

Among the many mysteries in the life of Maria Callas is the question of her date of birth. New documentation that we have found proves once and for all that she was born on December 2, 1923, at the Flower Hospital on Fifth Avenue in New York City.

She confirmed this in 1949 on her application for her Italian Identity Card at the municipal office in Zevio after her marriage to Meneghini. December 2 is also the given birth date on her American passport. Several other confirmations of this date can be seen on signed documents, the 1950 renewal of her U.S. passport in New York and later a letter renouncing her American citizenship, received by the American Consul Richard Kautsy in Paris on the eighteenth of March 1966; and eleven days prior to this, her application for renewal of her Greek citizenship sent to the Interior ministry in Athens. In Greece she was once again called Mariana Kalogeropoulos. In Athens she had supplied all the necessary documents required for citizenship including a birth certificate dated December 2, 1923.

At this time Callas was still hoping to become Mrs. Onassis and needed her Greek citizenship. According to the Greek Orthodox Church her marriage to Meneghini was void. Maria's official name in America, at least for the bureaucracy, was Sophie Cecilia Kalos.

According to her mother, her date of birth was December 4, which was not reliable, as she had not even bothered to register it. The school register gives her date of birth as December 3.

She always celebrated her birthday on December 2, and the testimonial of her godfather Doctor Lautzounis, who was present at the hospital at the time of her birth and had been the first person to see the baby Maria confirms this.

In her memoirs, Evangelia said, "One could say the life of my daughter started with a storm; something that shouldn't surprise anyone seeing that Maria's life has always been distinctly tempestuous. There was a terrible snowstorm on the day she was born; I've never seen anything like it. I had only been in America four months having just arrived from Greece and we never see anything like that in my country. I remember hearing the snow lashing against the window of the Flower Hospital and seeing Central Park all white."

When Maria was brought to her mother, she did not even look at her, turning her eyes away and staring out of the window at the snow covered park. She wanted a boy, not a girl. She already had a daughter Jakinty (Jackie) and her only son Vasily had died a few months previously at only three years of age. Evangelia and her husband Georges Kalogeropoulos, trying to forget this loss, had immigrated to America: They lived across the east river from Manhattan in Astoria, Queens. It was Doctor Lautzounis who gave the news to the unhappy mother that, "the nurses have not been able to put any of her baby clothes on her, she's big, as big as a lamb, six kilos and tall. She's got beautiful eyes and will be a heartbreaker."

It was three years before she was baptized in the Greek-Orthodox Cathedral on East Sixty-fourth Street in Manhattan and after much heated discussion they agreed on the names; Sofia Cecilia Anna Maria Kalogeropoulos, a name that the parents soon changed to Kallas as no one in America would be able to pronounce the real surname. Even though she had all those names she was always called simply, Maria.

Maria started walking at nine months and said her first words at eleven months. As was the habit in Greece, her mother breast-fed her for the first twelve months.

Jackie, her sister, had a lovely voice according to her mother and at the age of six sang very prettily. Evangelia was pleasantly surprised when one day while in the kitchen making bread, she heard Maria, who was only four years old at the time, playing the pianola without ever having had any instruction. And what is more, she moved her hands over the keys and was singing and had a strange light in her eyes; at the time, though pleased, Evangelia did not think that her daughter was special.

Maria always had an insatiable appetite: her mother recalls that she would fill herself up with bread, milk and *maccheroni*. She adored onions fried in butter, minced meat and tomatoes and was good at preparing a dish that she had invented: two fried eggs covered with fresh cheese known in Greece as Kasseri and when this wasn't enough, she would run into the kitchen and cook a few potatoes.

Evangelia was only persuaded that Maria's voice was out of the ordinary when she started to sing along with her canary Stefano: she loved to sing duets with him and imitated his chirping and trilling, so much so that she asked for another. This one she called David and they became a trio. At this point her mother decided to let her take singing lessons. Her first teacher was an Italian woman called Signorina Sandrina; Maria sang so loudly that one day a crowd gathered outside the studio and at the end of her song burst into applause. She sang everywhere; in the local church and anywhere else she might be. In all probability she had inherited her voice from her maternal great-grandfather Colonel Petros Dimitroadis who had been an officer in the Balkan war and could quite possibly with his fine tenor voice, had been a professional singer. Her great-uncle Dimitrios was also a great music lover and was highly considered in the family as he was close to King Constantine II. Her maternal grandmother was considered one of the most beautiful women in all of Greece and had even been compared to Helen of Troy. Another family phenomenon was her uncle Konstas, a charming young man who was a poet and had been published. Unhappily he committed suicide at the age of twenty-one.

Maria's first public appearance was at age eleven on an amateur hour-broadcast by the national radio station WOR. She sang "La Paloma" and "The heart is free," winning the first prize, a beautiful Bulova watch that she cherished and wore proudly for many years.

After moving to Washington Heights in upper Manhattan, Maria and her sister would sing at the church of St. Spyridon.

From an early age she also sang at countless school concerts and recitals.

Maria also loved acting and at the age of twelve she sang and acted in a performance of Gilbert and Sullivan's *The Mikado,* performing in a Japanese kimono made for her by her mother. She had other successes on the radio, always doing well in the competitions. Probably the only true recording we have of that period is the aria "O mio babbino caro," recorded at the age of twelve; its authenticity is unquestionable as it came from her home in Paris and was cherished by her till her death. The recording may have been of one of these radio broadcasts or made at one of the local studios that were common at that time and could be found around the Port Authority at Forty Second Street and Eighth Avenue in the Broadway area. It cost only a few cents and you could take home a 78-rpm vinyl recording of your own voice.

What has been proved as false is the much written about recording of "Un bel di vedremo" that Callas was said to have recorded under the name of Nina Foresti at about the same age. This piece by Puccini is preceded by a brief interview and even the noted writer and Callas expert John Ardoin found similarities in the voice. It was Callas herself who denied that it was she as soon as the tape started making the rounds in 1968 in a signed letter to a friend and admirer Olive Haddock of Leeds in England. Maria's actual words are:

Dear Olive,
I thank you for your love as usual and I will write more lengthy soon – I wrote a letter a while ago but I received no reply. Did you get it?
    I think of you all with such affection and hope soon to see you.
    The Butterfly piece is not true – I always called myself by my own name.
    Please write and forgive my long silences, you know me by now.
    Yours truly
    Maria

One only has listen to it to: The voice on the tape is shrill and lacking in grace and even the conversation is too "adult." It is odd that someone, as expert and close to Callas as John Ardoin, should endorse it and release it on CD. Her sister, in her book *Sisters*, mentions more facts of Maria's vocal progress:

> Maria spent hours singing either accompanying herself on the piano or I would sometimes play for her. Her usual repertoire was "La Paloma" or another song called "The heart is free," a charming waltz.

At the same time that Maria was studying with Signorina Sandrina she was introduced to another teacher, a Swede who was also a neighbor and friend of her mother. He gave Maria two months of free lessons and apparently the progress was deemed significant. Even though Jackie was Evagelia's favorite, it was at this point that she decided to dedicate herself with all the resolve she could muster in getting her second daughter's future secured. After another month of lessons, a newspaper article appeared like a bolt out of the blue, asking for young children to take part in a talent competition to be broadcast on the radio. After first running into some difficulties, Maria was accepted and as I have already mentioned, won the first prize competing against various other children telling jokes and displaying other talents. Evangelia exclaimed: "The inheritance of Grandpa the tenor!" Unquestionably Maria was talented and from that day on she was made to sing, sing, sing. Even though her role in the Mikado was small, for Evangelia it was a landmark in her daughter's career. The family was always glued to the radio and Maria first heard opera this way. Rosa Ponselle, who impressed her greatly in *Carmen* and Lily Pons, the light soprano famous at that time and acknowledged queen of the Metropolitan opera, were her favorite singers. Whenever the arias were broadcast Maria would sing along with Pons as she had done with her canaries, and managing to sustain all the notes, even singing higher with her still untrained voice. Her musicality and capacity to criticize had grown greatly and one day, listening to Lily Pons on the radio singing Lucia, she amazed the family by pointing to the radio during one of the cadenzas in the mad scene and exclaiming with disillusionment and anger that the great singer was singing flat! A family friend who was present tried to shut her up reminding her that Lily Pons was a great star and the infallible Idol of the Americans. Maria replied, "It doesn't matter that she is a star. Just wait and see: I'll also be a star." Her mother remembers this as Maria's first haughty gesture as a prima donna.

Maria attended school at PS 189 at 188th street and Amsterdam Avenue and on January 28, 1937 her mother and sister were packing their bags to return to Greece. It was also Maria's graduation day, one of the days that linger in one's memory forever. She had finished her eighth year of schooling and this was a final goodbye. Her scholastic record had not been brilliant but she had managed to pass all her exams and she had a talent that none of her companions had: her voice. The day's activities included singing and Maria, the future star, had the chance to surprise her schoolmates and be admired and applauded with enthusiasm; she had always been aloof and introverted and did not take part in the games they all played. She had no one to confide in, to tell her secrets and ambitions to and had never made any friends, nor did she really know how.

The highlight of the Graduation day was her singing; even at the rehearsal she had caused a stir and created quite a sensation. Once again she chose Gilbert and Sullivan the authors of her first scholastic success in the *Mikado*. This time it was the aria from *H.M.S. Pinafore*. At first she was a bit awkward and seemed nervous but as soon as she opened her mouth to sing it was wonderful. The applause was immense and she was asked to encore the piece. Her signature can still be seen in the yellowed pages of the yearbook of PS 189 along with customary notes written by everyone. Her companions had written brilliant and amusing thoughts summarizing their recollections of the time past together; she had no idea of what to write and simply wrote, "Being no poet, having no fame, permit me just to sign my name, signed *Mary Ann Callas*."

With this concert Maria left the school and ended her general education. In February of 1937, the tickets to Greece having been paid for by Georges, Evangelia and Maria said goodbye to her father and embarked on the Italian liner the *Saturnia* bound for Patras. Jackie had left earlier and would meet them in Athens. Her mother, for the good of her daughter, had made the decision to return to Greece where she would be able to take care of her musical education more inexpensively than in New York. This decision had been one of the causes of the growing remoteness between her and her husband who did not love opera on the whole and considered Maria's lessons a foolish and unnecessary expense. Evangelia's family in Greece was well connected in musical circles and she was sure she would be able to continue Maria's education keeping the cost to a minimum. Along with the two ladies, the three canaries were taken along, the third being Elmina a new acquisition who did not sing. Maria did not stay in her cabin for long but found the pianoforte in the salon and made it her home singing *La Paloma* and the *Ave Maria*. The Captain, making his inspection one day, heard her and asked her to sing at Mass. She refused but immediately accepted his invitation to sing at a party he had planned for the first-class passengers including three Italian countesses. Her mother dressed her in a blue frock with a white collar, and with her face powdered and removing her glasses, she had all the presence of a real performer who'd given concerts all her life. She had just turned thirteen. One of the pieces she sang was the Habanera from *Carmen*.

At the end while singing "Et si je t'aime prends garde à toi," instead of throwing a rose to Don Jose, Maria picked a carnation from a nearby vase and threw it to the Captain. He took it, laughed and kissed it. After the recital he gave her a bouquet of flowers and a doll that Maria immediately got rid of, probably throwing it out of the cabin porthole; no one ever saw it again. She had never had a doll . . .

On arrival at Patras, Callas and her mother were seen off the liner with full honors by the Captain and crew and continued their journey to Athens by train where Maria met her mother's music-mad family for the first time. According to Evangelia, her grandfather had at one time been the richest man in Greece and a fanatical melomaniac; the aunts, Pipitza, Sophia and Katia, were all good sopranos who loved to sing accompanying themselves on the guitar and mandolin; and Evagelia's three brothers also had good voices. As a result none of them thought she was out of the ordinary, rather, that her mother had overestimated her talent somewhat. Only her uncle Efthemios was in agreement that she should have lessons and, for the surprisingly unusual power of her voice, thought her superior to Jakie who did not take kindly to this opinion. "I like her," he said, "she's not afraid of anything. She's born to sing. Give her some time and I'm sure something good will come of it and then I'll organize an audition."

Her mother quickly found an apartment at number 61 Patission Street, comfortable, modern, and, naturally, with a piano.

The promised audition was organized for September 1937 and Maria Trivella, a teacher at the Ethnikon conservatory of music who was to play a significant role in the life of Maria Callas, was the judge.

The whole family was nervously waiting for the answer while Maria carried on calmly, a born actress. When the time came to sing for Madam Trivella, Maria was as calm as she had been singing for the Captain of the liner and his guests. On concluding the audition the teacher who had become quite flushed with enthusiasm shouted: "By Jove, this is a talent! She will become a great artist, I promise."

Taking Maria under her wing she taught her music and the rudiments of vocal technique as well as French and Greek which, although it was her native language, she spoke badly. Trivella also got her a study grant, lying about her age and saying she was sixteen instead of thirteen. Maria threw herself into her studies and her persistence surprised even her mother.

During the two years she studied with her, Madam Trivella became like a second mother; she was patient, sweet and gentle with her and Maria gave her one of the first pictures taken of her in Athens with a poignant dedication penned by the aspiring young singer. When she didn't eat her meals with Trivella, her mother would prepare her dinner and bring it to her on a tray so she could eat it on her knees without interrupting her studies. The next significant meeting she had was with George Karakandas, a famous teacher at the academy who taught her acting for years. She continued to learn from David, her canary, watching every movement of his throat, trying to discover his secrets, trilling and chirping for hours till she was worn out. One day, while singing a very high note in *Lucia di Lammer-*

moor, she had her revenge on her mute canary Elmina; she fell off her perch stunned by the vibrations and from then on was moved to another room when Maria was singing.

Nineteen thirty-eight was the year that Callas made her official debut, on April 11 of that year, in the final concert of Trivella's opera students at the Ethnikon Odeon. This first round of studies served to clarify one persistent question: was she a soprano or a mezzo-soprano?

After having developed the entire range, from a strong low and middle register, she also had the full range of high notes. She had tried both repertoires, studied all the scales and exercises and the final opinion was that she was a soprano. This was the decision of her teacher but quite likely also her own as she had put all her hard work into the soprano repertoire and had sincere aspirations to being a prima donna. For a girl of only fourteen the arias chosen by Trivella were certainly not easy. Agatha's aria from *Der Freischütz* by Weber, "Plus grand dans son obscurité" from Gounod's *Queen of Sheba*, "Two nights" by Ioannis Psaroudas and the duet from *Tosca* with the trained tenor Iannis Kabanis, one of Trivella's pupils. There is no known critical review or personal comment accessible regarding that performance. The first known review is from 1939 and is written by Ioannis Psaroudas, one of the composers chosen by Callas in her Ethnikon recital. The name she used in this period was her required Greek name Marianna Kaloieropulu and was used on her contracts and the posters for the performances. Psaroudas's review published in the Elefteron Vima, refers to the *Cavalleria Rusticana* performed on April 2, 1939, at the Olympia theater:

> Appearing for the first time in public in *Cavalleria Rusticana* if I remember correctly were Hilda Guntley and Miss. Kaloieropulu (in the second performance), both are worthy of praise for their efforts and both sang the difficult role of Santuzza with beautiful voices and were applauded warmly.

No mention was made of the danger of this role for the voice of a fifteen-year-old girl, one of the most technically risky, exposed and tiring in all opera. On May 22, 1939, at the Parnassos Hall, Marianna again sang a piece by Psaroudas: the aria "I'll never forget you." At the end of a concert that included Rezia's aria, "Ocean, thy mighty monster" from Weber's *Oberon*, "Ritorna vincitor," from *Aida,* the "Barcarole" from the *Tales of Hoffman* and the final duet "O terra addio" also from *Aida*, Psaroudas reiterated the fact that Kaloieropulu had one of the most beautiful voices for all types of music.

"I'm sure," he continued, "that with the right study and guidance from her teacher she will acquire the homogeneity that sometimes is wanting." In the same month, at the final concert of the academy students Psaroudas reviewed her again, this time less glowingly. "I must say that she was a bit wanting in the mirror scene from *Thais*. This requires great flexibility, coquetry and a pinch of hedonism that I'm sure she will attain with time." No one, not even her most ferocious critics, could ever accuse her of laziness. She studied day and night to the point of fainting, forgetting even to eat (something that in her case is hard to believe!). In spite of her outstanding vocal talents, she may not have gone as far as she did, had she not been so committed and determined. She was greatly admired for her dedication by all the students at the conservatory as well as by her acting teacher Professor Georges Karakandas but Maria was indifferent; actually she did not even like Karakandas and her behavior towards her companions was distant; as her mother likes to remind us, she was aggressive and would remove her glasses and clench her fists and would come to blows if she thought her rights had been violated.

The Trivella era came to a close with the final concert of the academy on June 25, 1939 that included an assessment in acting. Elli Nikolaidou accompanied and Marianna sang arias from *Un ballo in Maschera* and her favorite opera, *Cavalleria Rusticana*. The critic this time was D.A. Chamudòpulos who wrote in the Proia: *She exposed vocal qualities and the talent to use them with creative expression.*

To my darling teacher to whom I owe all. Mary Anna. The dedication that Maria inscribed on a photograph to her teacher where she looks even younger than fifteen. The same words were used again in a peremptory and definitive fashion to the great Elvira De Hidalgo, who was about to enter Maria's life. A crucial meeting.

Maria Trivella did however make an impression on the first years of Callas' musical education as one can see from the reviews of the period. Here is the text translated faithfully from Greek of a letter Trivella wrote to Evangelia Kalogeropoulos at the end of the 1960s:

> Dear Mrs. Kalogeropoulos, in reply to your question and for the sake of the truth, I am happy to uncover some facts that, maybe, have been kept hidden too long from the public and whomsoever is interested in the life of the great artist that Maria Callas is. I remember the day in 1937 when little Maria accompanied by her uncle Taki Dimitriades and my brother-in-law Stephanos Trivella came to me for an audition and a few vocal exercises. I accepted her gladly and was excited about the potential that her voice had to offer. After a year of daily lessons, I noted that her voice had developed wonderfully and decided to let her sing in the annual concert and allow her to sit the entrance exam for our conservatory. As I had hoped and expected, she triumphed and won the first prize of the National Odeon. The next year we worked on opera arias and she made her debut in Cavalleria. When she won first prize for opera, I remember that she suggested that I award her the diploma without delay, I refused and replied with these words: *Let us wait another year. You have a wonderful instrument and we need to work on it a bit more.* And so Maria and I started our third year of work and we went on till 1939. I worked with her not only as a teacher but also with all the love and devotion of a mother. It was a great joy to teach her as today I have the satisfaction of knowing I contributed to a glorious future. Maria with her never resting ambition was predestined to

scale the heights and I am happy she made it. I have loved her and still do with all my heart. May she always be happy! May she always shine in the artistic firmament.

Maria Trivella had helped Callas to use a big and still rough inexpert voice, already capable when required of sweetness and agility and, in a way, also prepared her for her new life. Maria or Marianna or Mary as her name appeared on the posters had sung works in Italian, German, French, English, Spanish and Greek.

Times were changing and the stability of Greece was shaken by the events in neighboring Albania. On April 7, 1939 Mussolini's Italian troops occupied Albania. King Zog fled the country and Albania was annexed to Italy under the crown of Victor Emanuel III. Athens was not yet caught up in the conflict but would be within the next two years. At the end of June 1939 the historic and decisive meeting between Callas and the great Elvira De Hidalgo took place. It was a partnership that lasted six years and yielded her first professional engagements right up to the *Fidelio* at the amphitheater of Herod Atticus.

De Hidalgo herself tells the story of their first meeting in a fascinating portrait of the young Callas.

> Maria Callas was sixteen when we first met. It was preposterous to think that the girl wanted to be an opera singer. She was very tall and big and wore heavy glasses. If she removed them, she would look at you – but obviously she couldn't see you: big eyes steady and feverish. All the rest was immobile and seemed quite immovable. Her dark hair was in two braids wound around her ears and on her head was a white cap. She wore a school apron and worn out sandals on her feet. She sat in a corner and being unsure what to do with her hands, she started biting her nails. This she continued to do until her turn came to sing. She stood up and came over to me walking heavily and swinging side to side. Her round face covered in pimples caused by excessive childish greed.

Appearance: Hopeless.

One hot afternoon at the end of 1939 we were at the Athens conservatory: The young Callas was on the list as Marianna Caloyeropulos. "We'll get nothing out of this one." I thought to myself. Then without a word of warning she started to sing. Thinking about it now makes me smile because every one now knows who Maria Callas is: I however, discovered it at that moment. All of a sudden I felt alert and tense. That voice, the voice I had long been secretly searching and hoping for. It was as though a rendezvous had been kept with destiny. I closed my eyes. A violent, emotional, dramatic and uncontrolled flood of sound poured out, difficult to explain in simple words without getting into technical language.

She would have to start all over again but I was happy to have the opportunity to mould such amazing raw material. On opening my eyes again, I once again saw this large girl whose appearance was so hopeless. I told her that she had been accepted and could join the non-fee paying classes. She returned to her seat and continued to bite her nails. When I told her she could leave, she replied Thank you and remained there till all the applicants had finished singing. Later this conduct became a habit: Marianna Caloyeropulos arrived first at lessons and was the last to leave. Often she would wait for me and walk beside me on the way home.

The next five years, from the time of her audition to the time she left for America trying to patch up the rift that had come between us (I will explain later), were the most important in the life of this great Greek singer.

Why should I, born in Spain, widowed by an Italian and remarried to a Frenchman, used to singing Rosina, Violetta and Lucia at San Carlo in Naples, La Scala or at the Metropolitan, owner of homes in Milan and Paris – have to be stuck here in Greece all that time? One could answer: To meet Maria Callas. I sometimes thought so too, but these are the facts.

Every year I would go to Athens to sing a short season and then do a tour visiting Thessalonica and Volos. The war broke out in 1939 and my way home was cut off. Fortuitously I had friends in Athens. The director of the conservatory had always inundated me with calls and invitations to accept a teaching post and this time I was happy to oblige, so, here I was Professor of singing and stage direction at the Athens Conservatory. Later I was also appointed to the board of the recently founded State Opera along with the famous Paxinou and her husband, the actor Minotis and the writer Bastias, the right hand man of Metaxas.

From the first day of my working with Callas I realized that she was on the wrong path. Born, as we know, in the United States of America, she had been forced by her mother to be a child prodigy. Even though she undoubtedly had a sincere and deep vocation, all those competitions, done at an early age, had left her with a sense disgust and resentment for depriving her of a proper childhood. In 1937 she had arrived in Athens with her mother and sister both originally from Greece and had remained there. She had entered into the routine of piano and singing lessons at the other conservatory, the *National* where she had been accepted by faking her age by three years. When she heard that I would be teaching at The Athens conservatory, by far the better of the two, she presented herself at the audition I have already mentioned.

Music, pastries and ice cream.

She was not content to limit herself to studying and had made her debut in the role of Santuzza in Cavalleria Rusticana. True madness.

Apart from her obvious immaturity, the poor Santuzza had severe toothache that had caused her face to swell up.

Not to mention the end result: but Callas as a student was the finest I'd ever had. I had noticed right from the first audition, the first lesson, that she had a gift few others have; an extraordinary musical memory. Without this ability to learn a piece of music at a glance she would have had great difficulty getting ahead. The fact that she was extremely nearsighted was instrumental in developing this talent, as without her glasses, she could not even see the conductor or follow his beat. To this day Callas does not look at the conductor; it would be futile.

She concentrates on her music and with the notes and her amazing intuition and not the maestro's baton, she would give the attacks. Marianna Caloyeropulos would arrive each morning at ten o'clock and would stay till late in the evening listening to all the lessons I gave and in this way, almost without realizing it, learned a vast repertoire of works. She had three passions in life: Music, pastries and ice cream. All three were a substitute for everything she missed.

Her Mother and sister Jackie were quite different; dressing up to look attractive, going to the theater and parties, entertaining friends. Maria stayed at home to study and take care of the house. It might be extreme but not far from the truth to call her a sort of "Cinderella." Consequently, she had no idea about social graces but could cook very well and as a result of her greediness, got fat.

Evidently I would have to "reinvent" her and relished the idea jumping at the opportunity with great energy, much to the merriment of my other pupils who would exclaim, Who is that rag-doll?

When I asked her to wear something more elegant to a recital, she arrived wearing a dress of two violently contrasting reds,

Unfortunately her size made the whole thing rather comic. As with her voice, her choice of colors was excessive. Having astonishing breath control and being able to sing an entire piece in one breath and a natural ability to dramatic inflection, she was inclined to blow on her breath and get it all out quickly. The first bit of advice I gave her was to slow down. "You're young," I explained, "and for now you will have to get used to singing lightly, like embroidery. Later on, we'll see."

I made her cry.

After lessons, walking home through the war-darkened streets of Athens, I would reprimand her, pulling at her terrible clothes and tell her that I was not happy with her progress and would point out every little defect that I found. Almost every night she would burst into tears and holding onto my arm would ask through the tears, "What do I have to do to make you say that I'm doing well?"

I don't enjoy talking about the war years; they were atrocious. I will only say that so as not to die of hunger and cold, Maria would have to walk for miles across the muddy countryside: returning home with a basket of tomatoes or a bundle of cabbage leaves. For a time she also worked in an office at an Italian military base.

I sometimes gave lessons to the soldiers from the base, most of them, being from the southern regions of Italy, fancied themselves tenors and would pay with loaves of bread. While the Italians were in charge things got noticeably better. Occasionally a few officers would arrive with a truck and take my students away to sing concerts for the soldiers in Athens, Thessalonica and Volos paying them with kilos of spaghetti, butter, sugar and macaroni.

In order to save Maria from any further unnecessary distractions and to let her earn her living I decided to help. I took her to the hairdresser, the manicurist and the dressmaker. When I presented her to the members of the board, no one recognized her. She walked on stage and I overheard the other pupils say, "Look how well she moves." The transformation was staggering. When she had finished singing I told the committee, You have to give this girl a job, pay her a salary, engage her as a chorister but she must not sing. She must have an income and only study, no singing. We must protect this treasure or she will waste her time singing for soldiers for a crust of bread. My advice was taken and only when she was twenty-one did I allow her to sing Tiefland and Fidelio. Later, for the same reason I acted quite the opposite: to make Maria Callas into a great singer.

In 1945 we had an regrettable rift in our relationship. How? In Italian, the language I had taught her and she with her extraordinary ability and on a bet, had learned to speak in only three months.

Why? At the end of the war Maria wanted to go to America, to see her father and have a more comfortable life while starting her career there. I was against this move. "You must start in Italy," I explained. "That is why you learned the language. When you have become somebody in Italy the rest will follow." Maria did not listen. She left alone and with no money on the Ocean liner Stockholm. On the evening of her departure she called me. "My last words are for you," she said. "I will always think of you with gratitude. Tell me you forgive me." "You must not leave," I repeated.

I want your jewels.

    Shortly afterwards an influential Athenian made a generous offer: That extraordinary pupil of yours he said, "The one going to America, she interests us. She could be a national treasure. What will it take? We want to help with a large sum of money, perhaps to get her started." "It is not needed," I replied. "Wherever she goes, whatever she does, in whatever circumstances she finds herself in, Maria Callas will manage. She has the strength of a river in her and no one can stop the flow of a river. It is good that an artist suffers, encounters difficulties, goes hungry."

    I knew that Maria was more than just a singer: she was a complete artist.

    Callas herself knew this. Today one hears repeated often that when she arrived in Italy she was no one and only after her marriage to Meneghini was she able to complete her education. These are bogus and absurd affirmations; no one knows better than I.

    I will only quote from a few of the hundreds of letters Callas wrote to me from all over the world. I feel they will be a useful testimonial. In one of them she writes, *I will never forget you. What a pity that you can't see me on stage. I hope I do justice to a teacher like you… if you have any suggestions. (I'm sure you have many.) please write to me. Your precious advice will take me to all the places we both dreamed of.*

    Another, from America in 1946: *You were right when you told me the Metropolitan is no longer what it used to be. I thank you for having given me this method of singing… I will try to remember all the things you taught me always…*

    Contrary to what he has said in recent interviews, this is what Meneghini wrote to me from Verona: *If Maria has earned herself a prominent place and a name, she owes it all entirely to you.*

    Lastly, again from Maria, this time from Italy: *I want to ask you a big favor. I wanted to ask before and did not have the courage but now I feel I am worthy. I would like to have your stage jewelry. It is more a moral satisfaction than other. I will be filled with pride and happiness to be able to wear the jewels of De Hidalgo on stage. Don't you think I am the only person who could inherit them?*

With extraordinary foresight Teodoro Celli wrote, Callas' voice "is from another time." It does, in effect, have all the characteristics of a vocal instrument of another age. In all probability she sings the way singers did over a hundred years ago, or at least approaches the way we have been led to believe they sang. The soprano roles in certain operas by Rossini, Donizetti, Bellini and the early works of Verdi were written for musical instruments, a very rare event today and one that Callas' voice

MARIA CALLAS
Divina

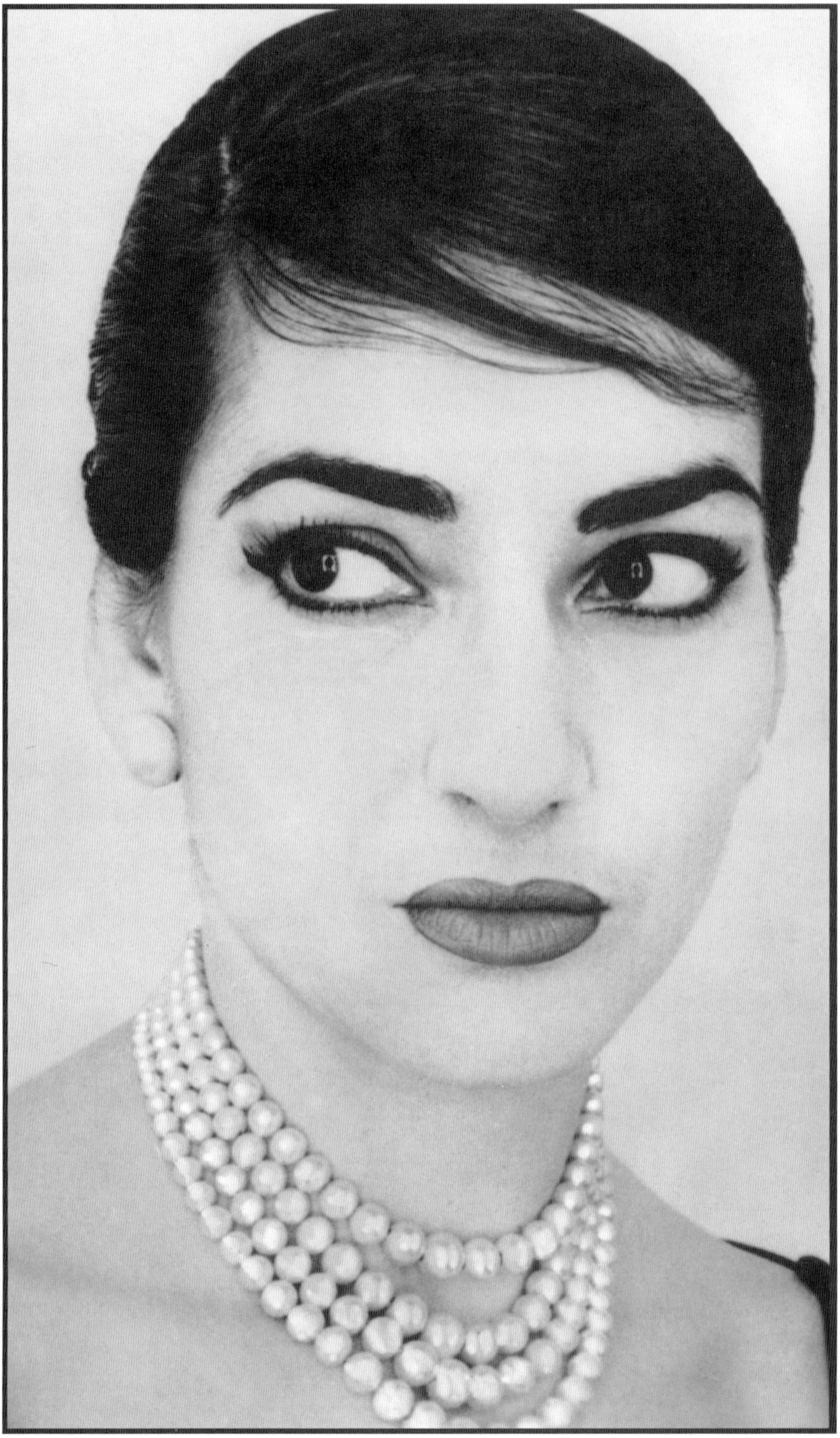

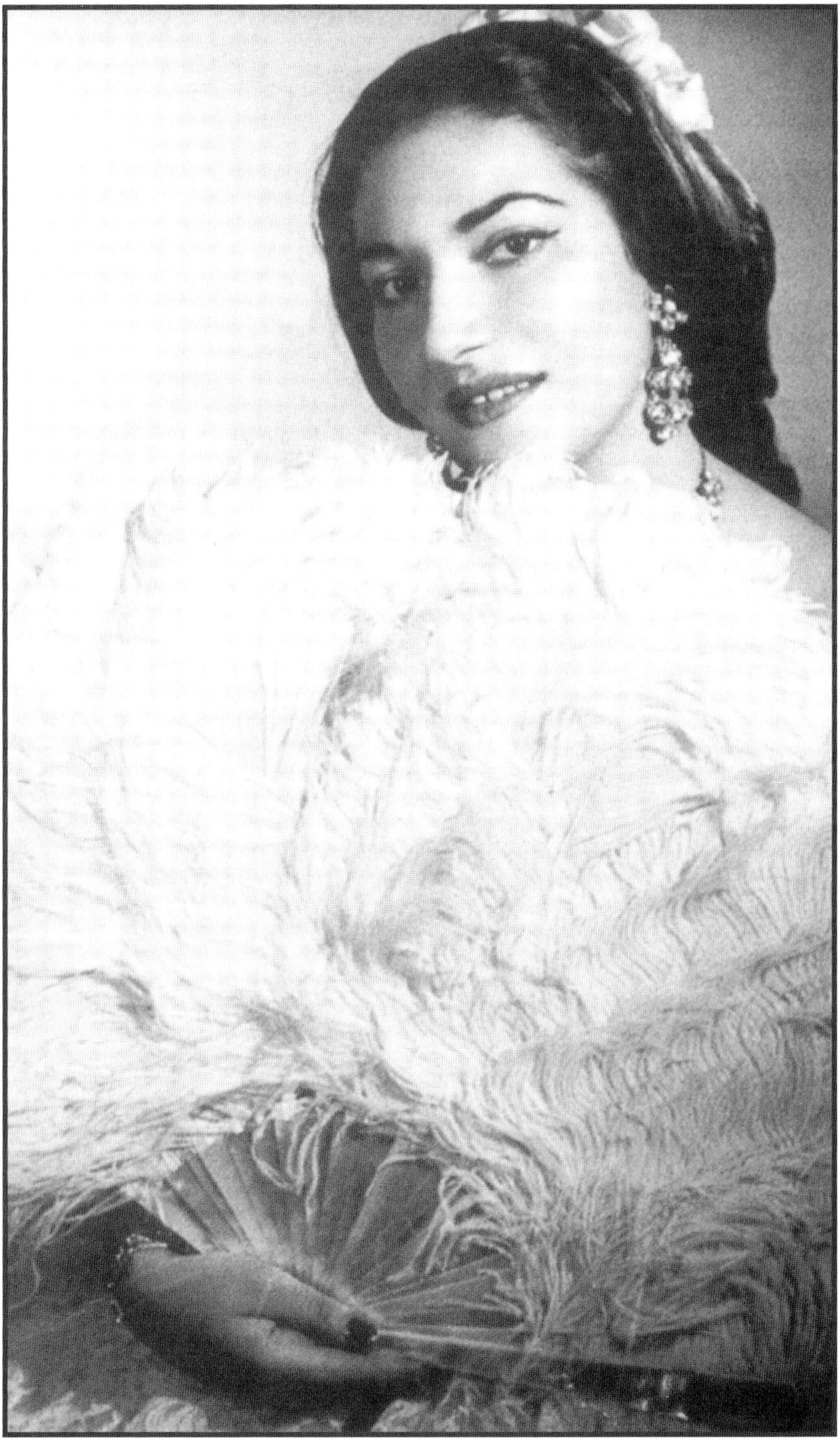

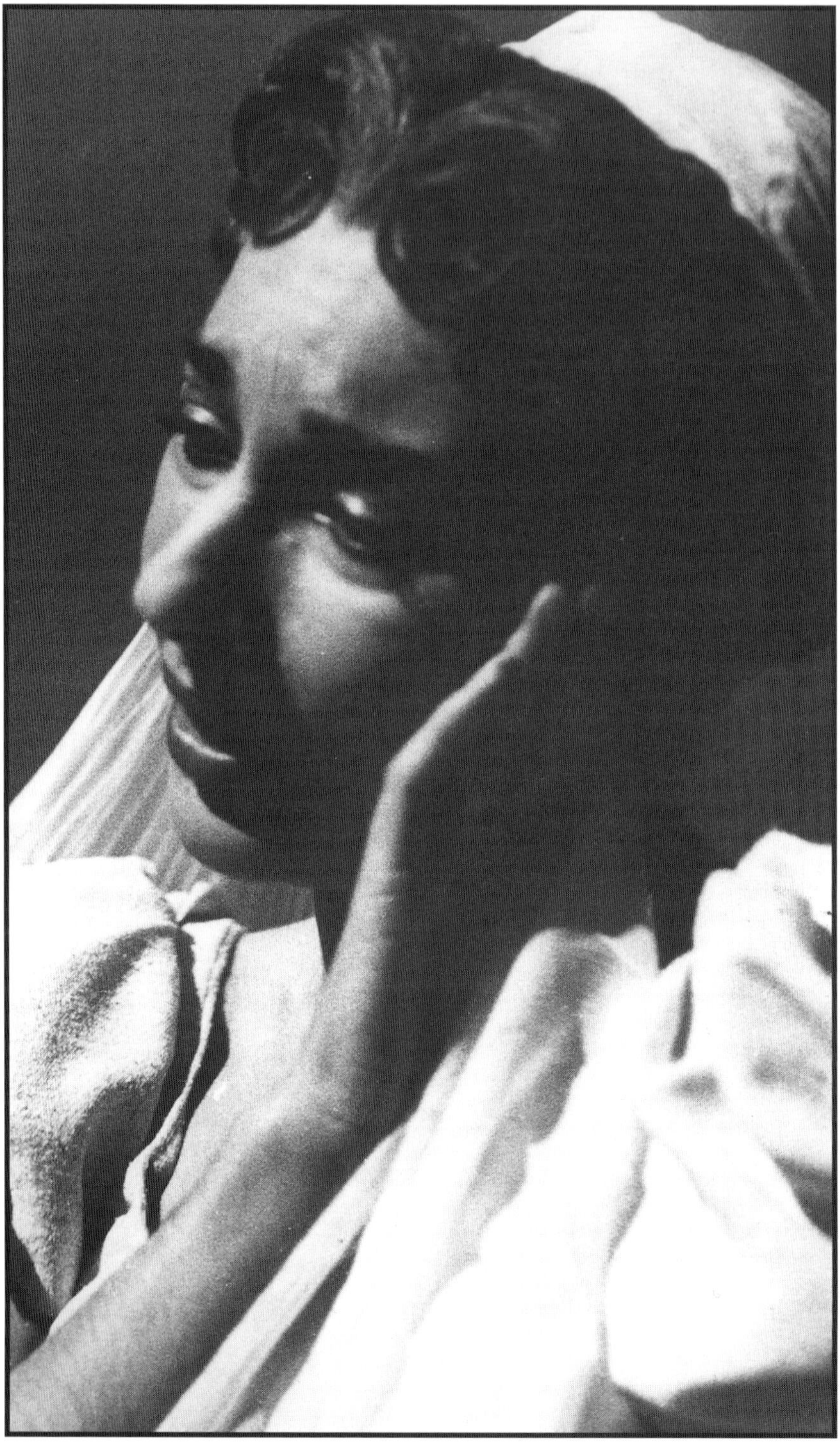

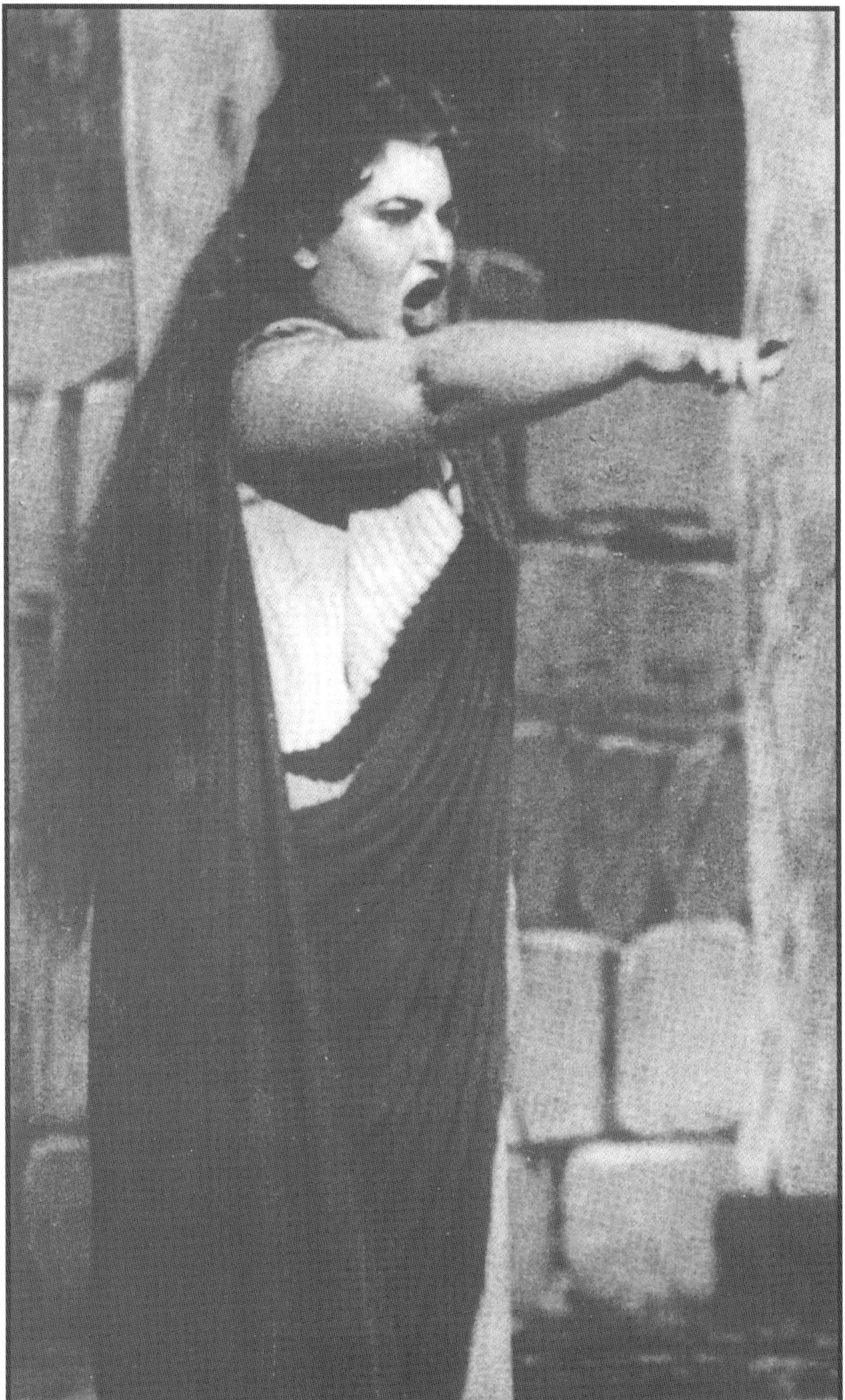

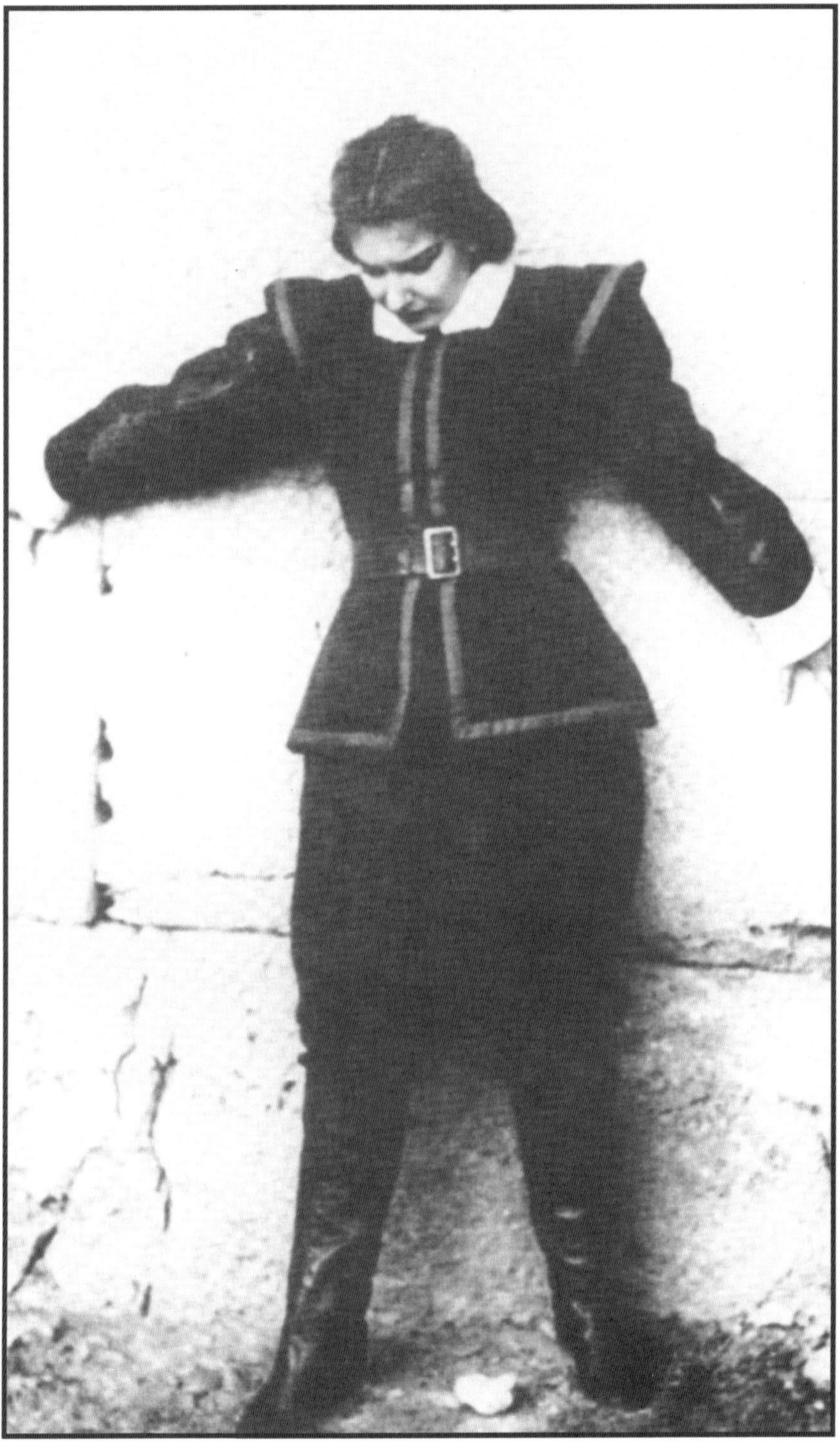

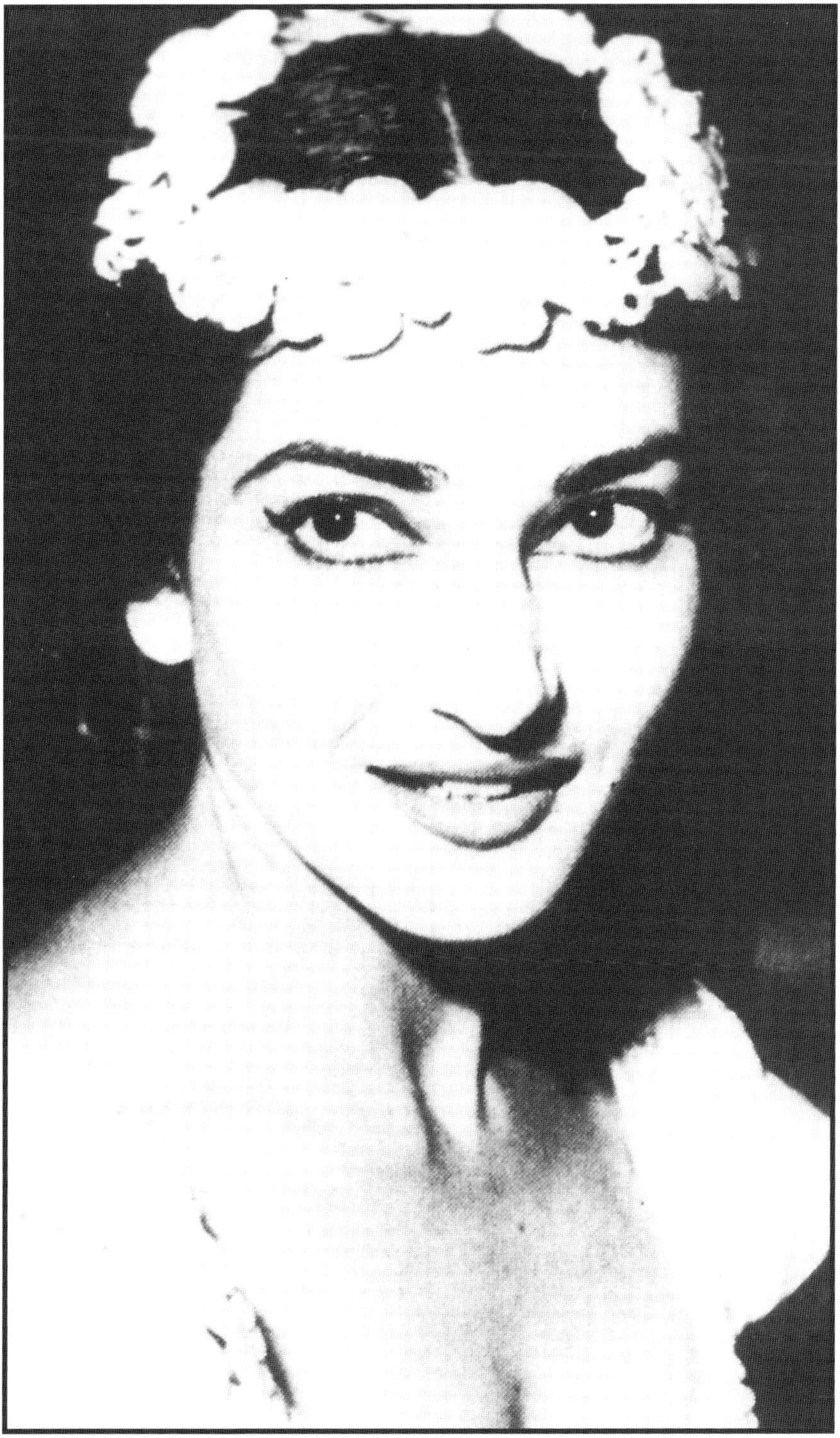

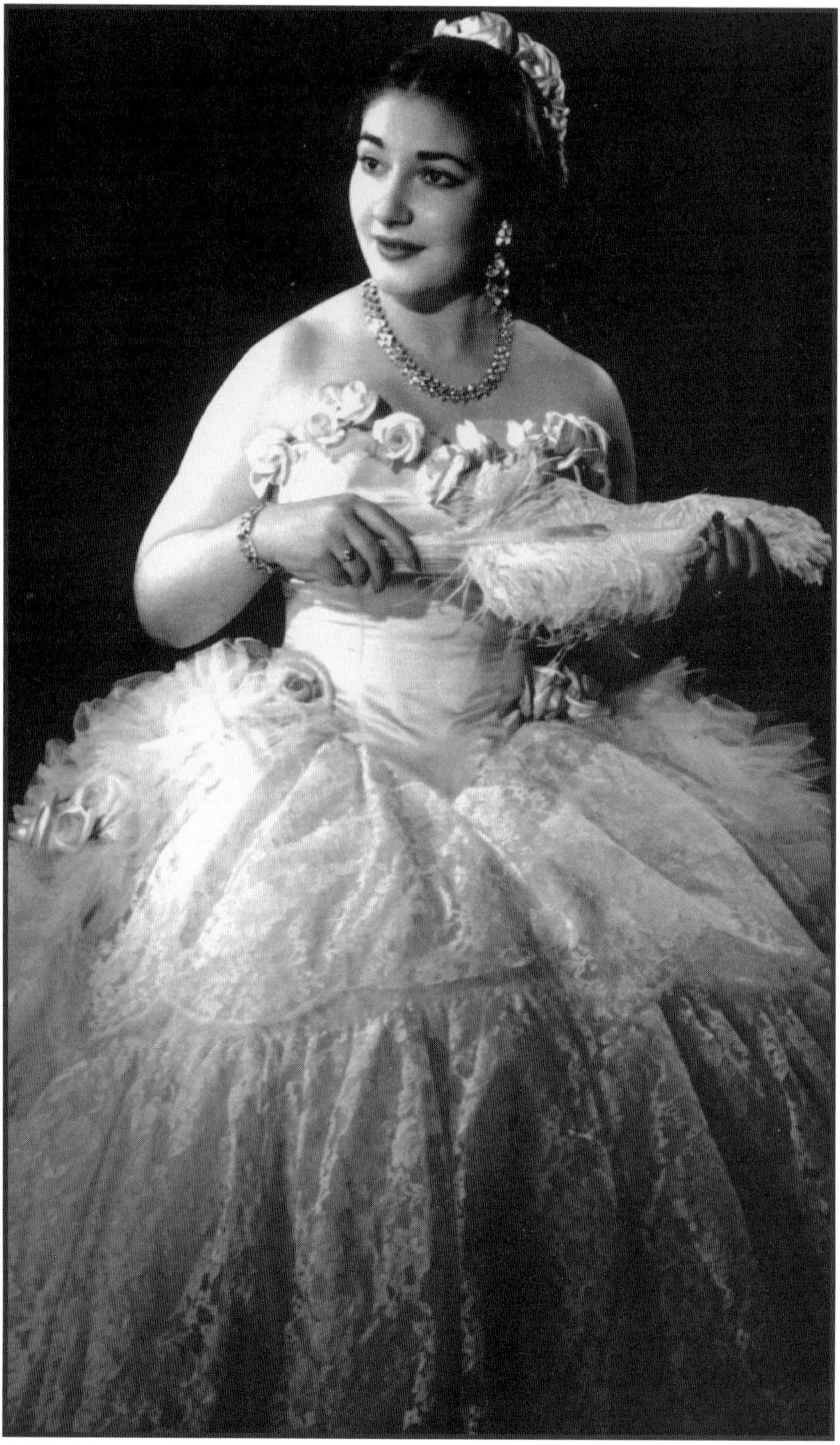

would seem to be the closest approximation. When she applied her musical instrument to the most apposite repertoire and to those dramas that required the subtle poetic understanding that she was so blessed with, not only was she compelling in her singing but an interpreter of exceptional and affecting efficiency. All this without taking into account that the power and extension of her voice in her early years is almost without precedent. Her vocal extension was from A flat below middle C to the high E flat and even to the high E as used in *Armida* at the *Maggio Musicale* in Florence. The fact that she studied with Elvira De Hidalgo, a great light soprano and heir to the secrets of "Canto fiorito" (Florid singing) was instrumental in Callas' repeating the work done by singers in the early part of the nineteenth century such as Malibran (whom one is obliged to compare her with), to blend the contralto voice to that of the soprano and to accentuate the more *impassioned* agility. Because of the inequality in the timbre of her voice that on hearing for the first time could be perplexing, Callas took a long time to be acknowledged. Someone likened her voice to a not very good piano being played by a great pianist. By hard work and most certainly the vigorous and advantageous instruction of De Hidalgo, Callas was able to gain complete control and improve the natural timbre of her voice that in the beginning was an avalanche of sound, a force of nature of enthralling capabilities. De Hidalgo provided her with the means to lighten her sound, to develop her full extension and to alternate the dramatic thrust with the agility of the light soprano like no other singer in our times has been able to achieve.

Her professional career started in Greece under the guidance of De Hidalgo. In 1942 she sang the small role of Beatrice in *Boccaccio* performed at the Pàllas Cinema and later in the open-air Park Theater. She also sang the open-air *Tosca* that was repeated the following year in 1943 and in

1944 various concerts of varied and difficult arias. Finally in 1944 she sang the ground breaking roles of Martha in *Tiefland* where, for the first time, she was recognized for her dramatic instinct, intensity of expression and spontaneity in her acting and finally *Fidelio* at the amphitheater of Herod Atticus where the critics unanimously agreed that she was the preeminent young opera singer in Greece. It was a vain hope that her successes in Greece would be of help in launching a career in Europe and America as Greece, then and now, does not play an important role in the geography of world opera. What had proved to be of great importance were the six years spent with De Hidalgo who literally created the artist imparting all the knowledge that would be important to her in taking her first steps on the world stage. There were only two occasions when they had differences of opinion. One was in 1945 when Callas insisted on singing *Cavalleria Rusticana* again (the only time the Athens critics panned her) and when she decided to leave for America and try to start her career there, rather than listen to what her teacher had to say and start in Italy. Their relationship was intense and affectionate right to the end of Maria's life.

De Hidalgo died in 1980, living three years longer than Maria.

They exchanged hundreds and hundreds of letters and had scores of encounters. Donna Elvira would be with her often in her role of severe but affectionate controller and once more went to her in the seventies after the tours with Di Stefano and Callas wanted to get back onto the opera stage. We were able to view these fascinating letters that make up part of the collection belonging to Illario Tamassia, Maurizio Capusoni, and Bruno Antoniolli of Milan, who have allowed us to publish for the first time some of Callas' letters to her teacher.

In 1948 Callas sang her first *Aïda* in Turin. On September 30 she wrote to De Hidalgo, telling her about the experience and keeping her up to date on her progress, not without a stab at the critics who were questioning her Verdianità.

> My dear Madam,
> please excuse me for not writing earlier but I was busy with the preparations for Aida in Turin which went very well, (just as you thought) actually, it was a triumph . . . Now they say I am the Verdi voice. Poor fools, the more art is lacking, so even more with sound judgment. If it weren't for Serafin, I would never sing, according to them (the critics), I'd have to always scream as they say that it is impossible for a powerful voice to sing Verdi. They forget the voices of the past... and a conclusion worthy of Callassian charisma: Well, in the end I won and that's all that matters.

On October 6, 1948, De Hidalgo replied from Ankara by return of post.

> Brava, my Maria.
> I would have loved to be present at your triumph. I think the people of Turin still remember my Barber. I have never forgotten the ovations in the Regio Theater.
> Now you are tranquil and happy, you have won, as you say and look, the battle didn't last long. Think about the others, the humiliations and tears before achieving one third of what you have.
> You must thank God, smile on good fortune, be courteous to everyone and never forget the person you have beside you, that loves you dearly and is of great moral help, because he indirectly contributes to your success. Send him my kindest regards.
> I beg you, please write often and send me the newspapers. Brava once again, with an affectionate kiss.

Again from Ankara on January 3, 1949:

> Your telegram arrived on Sunday and I only received it in the evening. You can imagine how disappointed I was not to hear you on the radio.
> The newspapers I have seen filled me with joy. You see, Maria, I was not wrong, and the steps you took in Athens, without my consent did you no service, only slowed down the speed of the success you have had in Italy. Reading about your triumph, particularly in Norma that we had studied together so lovingly, moved me. Even though a bit late, the dream we had has

been realized. I wish that 1949 will bring you all the triumphs and satisfaction you deserve.

Another beautiful letter from Turkey dated March 15/18, 1949:

Dearest Maria,
First of all I must tell you how much it moved me to hear you on the "Turin" radio and then the next day in Rome in "Parsifal." Brava, Maria! As you can see, I was right when I told you not to listen to others because the way I taught you would allow you one day to sing any opera while the others told you at sixteen that you were a dramatic soprano. I made you sing "Cenerentola" and sing scales like a light soprano: that is why today you can astonish everyone singing "Puritani" and "Parsifal." I'm really proud of you. Here my students are crazy about you and ask for a photograph.

Here is a previously unpublished letter from Maria: evidently in answer to the above, announcing her marriage to Meneghini that was to take place the next day in the sacristy of the convent of the Filippini.

My dear Madam,
I'm writing a few words to thank you for your beautiful words. I am happy to have been able to make you proud of me. Now, in 4 days time I am embarking for Buenos Aires where I have a contract with the Colon. I had to accept "Turandot" for the last time because that way, they would also give "Norma" and probably Aida. I think I will arrive around May 14. If you write, you will make me happy – write to me at the Teatro Colon. And so I announce my good news. I'm marrying Battista. We decided because we love each other and understand each other like no one else. I know you will be happy because you told me about your husband.

My dear, write lots and I promise to do the same and send all the reviews. Let's hope they're good!
Look after yourself and write,
Your most affectionate.
Maria.

The P.S. is from Meneghini and written literally in the margins of the two sheets:

To the affectionate and mindful greetings of Maria, who remembers you with infinite devotion as the person who paved the way for her art and offered the riches of knowledge, I adjoin mine with reverent gratitude together with the announcement that as soon as possible, Maria and I will join our hearts and lives in marriage.

I remain your devoted. G.B. Meneghini.

Another letter from De Hidalgo:

Karanfil Sokak 15 b. Ankara, June 27, 1949.

Dearest Maria,

I received your letter from Buenos Aires together with the newspapers. Yesterday I received a letter from your husband telling me of the great enthusiasm the Argentinean public had for your "Norma." It is quite unnecessary to tell you how happy I am and how truly proud I am of you. I hope that now after your success, you will accept Brazil if it is offered: once you have undertaken such a long voyage it is best to collect as many honors and as much money possible.

I understand your desire to return to Italy and to your husband, who, from his letters, adores you. But an artist often has to make difficult sacrifices and I think that on this point you will be in agreement with me.

Many years later a letter from Callas to De Hidalgo announced that she had been "liberated" from a nightmare, from a "Destructive love" (Onassis):

Paris 3/10/68

Dear Elvira,

It has been a long time since I've written but I was very far away.

Traveling with dear friends across America and Mexico. You will have heard my news from Manolo. Nothing new. I am much better after my fall last month: The result, the cartilage of the second rib in my chest, broken. A long time healing – and very painful – annoying for a singer. We have to take life as it comes.

I'm very well and in good spirits. I've been freed of a nightmare that was a in every way a destructive love affair. I go out every night with friends and in a week I will be able to start studying again a little at a time.

Give hugs to all your family and if you get a chance call Manolo to send him my greetings. Also Biki.

I'm not leaving Paris till Christmas.
Lots of tender kisses from your joyful!
Maria.

So as not to disappoint her teacher, Maria signs the letter *Joyful Maria*. In truth, she was searching for a new direction. She had not sung since 1965 and would only start again in 1969 with a recording in February and in the summer with Pasolini's film, *Medea*. Filled with serenity and hope for the future she wrote to De Hidalgo on March 26, 1969 giving her news:

> Dear Elvira,
> A long time has passed since your last letter and I have so much to tell you (as usual). I had not written to thank you for your eternal affection. I'm well enough. Certainly I have my ups and downs. I'll make it – I must – I'm still young and the world looks on me as an example of integrity. Meanwhile, I've got stomach problems (too many sandwiches!) and this does not help my physical condition as I have a low globule count but I try to live with my faults and do the best I can. I'm almost sure to be doing the Medea film with Pasolini and I hope to God that it gives me satisfaction.
> I'm treating it as a diversion and a new door that (maybe) will be opened apart from keeping my singing alive. Meanwhile I have recorded one side of an LP (with EMI of Verdi arias from *I Lombardi, Attila* and *Il Corsaro*). I continue to practice and hope that the road will be smoother recognizing all that I have done with courage and constant work. How are you and what are you doing? I wanted to come to Milan but traveling right now is of little interest to me.
> I think of you often. I think about how much you suffer for my pain but also think with pride, that you admire my behavior and self-esteem. Elvira that is how I am made and I cannot change it. I am, as they say, a good woman and am proud of it but cannot console myself when I see the others making progress with such dubious talents.
> I embrace you my dearest,
> Your Maria.

There is an interesting account from the German journalist P.W. Herzog writing for the Athens "Deutsche Nachrichten" during the Nazi occupation stating that the career of the woman that he calls the Prima donna assoluta started in 1943 only due to the help of the German high command. Herzog also worked as music critic for this paper of which many examples exist and are quoted in Callas' biography (one of them being a beautiful review of *Fidelio*).

According to an article written by Herzog many years later after his return to Germany, Maria Callas owed much to the support of the German occupying forces that had overrun her country. Herzog says that when she was eighteen years old she had mobilized everyone to help her career but waited in vain for her compatriots' help, help that came instead from a most unexpected source: the Nazis. In an article that appeared in Hamburg in1959 (in the Information paper the organ of the ex-German war correspondents), he refers to the commander of the German troops in occupied Greece, General Wilhelm Spiedel, brother of a future NATO leader, who was passionate about opera and took every opportunity to try to help opera students and other Greek musicians.

Mariana Kalojoropoulos (as she was known), having American citizenship, should have been interned in a camp along with her mother. Young Maria had studied at the Athens Opera but had been disappointed by the fact that she had not been engaged by the theater. In spite of the protection of her teacher Elvira De Hidalgo, she had only been included in a few concerts. Her colleagues and compatriots did not like her particularly and treated her as an intruder in their quest for roles. Maria did not really do much to make them like her either. When she was finally awarded the part of Martha in D'Albert's *Tiefland* it was understood that it was only due to the intervention of the Germans. The Greek baritone Manelivaras, who sang the part of Sebastian, was according to Herzog, madly in love with Maria and said he would marry her at any cost. The reply was always an icy "no!" Even the contracts for *Tosca* and *Cavalleria Rusticana* were only obtained by the direct interest expressed by

General Spiedel in person. In September of 1944, only a few weeks before the evacuation of the German troops from Greece, the festival of classic opera was held in Athens. On the program was *Fidelio* by Beethoven with Kalojoropoulos in the lead role of Leonora. The direction of the opera was given to the famous Oscar Wallech, the head of the Prague Opera. Herzog writes:

> In *Fidelio* the Greeks had glimpsed the idea of the liberation; they understood at last that the tyranny and oppression of the enemy was at an end and that the final victory was in sight.
> When Maria sang Leonora's aria "Abscheulicher"... letting them feel the full power of her magnificent voice together with that of the tenor Delendas, the enthusiasm in the hall grew until it burst into a vast ovation that became true delirium. Callas' first success was a truly an unforgettable night.

Maria arrived in Italy for the first time on June 29, 1947: it was without a doubt an unforgettable journey given that she had all her hopes placed on what might have proven to be the one and only opportunity given to her to begin the career that was not going anywhere. *La Gioconda* was the opera that was to open the season at the Arena of Verona. After her first successes as a young singer in Greece she had tried without success to perform in America but was only rewarded with promises and disillusionment. An unscrupulous impresario had got as far as getting her to rehearse a *Turandot* in an old Broadway theater that came to nothing. The opportunity to sing *Butterfly* at the Metropolitan in 1946 also went up in smoke even though she got close. There were six other sopranos auditioning for the honor of wearing the costume of Cio-Cio-San on the most prestigious American stage. The judges and the general manager of the theater though recognizing her splendid voice did not find her entirely believable in the part. Callas had put on an inordinate amount of weight in the time she had been back in America and her bulky figure did not lend itself to the requirements of the American stage.

Maria had arrived in America on the Swedish liner the Stockholm at the end of September 1945 full of hope. She had traveled alone not wanting her mother on the trip and having had an argument with Elvira De Hidalgo who had tried to persuade her to change her mind and go to Italy which she considered the promised land for a singer with her talent.

After crossing the Atlantic and following a moving sighting of the Statue of Liberty, sure of herself and proud in her childish innocence that she had stood up to both her mother and her teacher, she disembarked not even knowing her father's address, intending to see her godfather Leonida Lantzounis, with whom she had corresponded regularly, and the bass Nicola Moscona who had encouraged and praised her to the highest degree in Athens and was now singing in New York with Toscanini. Her father, as was his habit, had been reading a Greek newspaper and had by chance noticed a Maria Kalogeropoulos on the passenger list of the Stockholm. On her arrival, to her great joy and surprise, she found him waiting for her. Maria went to live with him in his apartment on West 157th Street where she found a room prepared. She immediately started doing the rounds in the musical world with no luck.

De Hidalgo had suggested that she contact the teacher of the celebrated soprano Rosa Ponselle, Romano Romani who listened to her sing a few arias and said that she needed to work more than study and did no more to help her. Contrary to what she had been lead to believe, the bass Nicola Moscona did his best to avoid her and after eventually allowing her a brief meeting, refused to introduce her to Toscanini. The tenor Martinelli, one of the pillars of the Metropolitan, too said that she was not yet ready to sing in the big houses. There was no phone in the house and she had no piano.

By chance a friend introduced her to Louisa (Louise) Caselotti, a mezzo-soprano, and singing teacher of Italian origin who lived with her husband, a lawyer, Edward Richard Bagarotzy, also known as Eddie. She was invited to visit their home and to listen to some of Caselotti's pupils. She made friends with them and saw them often, one of the reasons being that she had made a favorable impression after singing a few arias. Nicola Rossi Lemeni was also a frequent guest and they started to put some ideas together. The United States Opera Company was founded in New York. At Bagarotzy's side as general manager was his partner, Ottavio Scotto, Italian agent and impresario lately of the Colon in Buenos Aires and the widower of the great soprano Claudia Muzio. Though not flush with funds, Bagarotzy and Scotto managed to put a company of excellent singers together among whom the already well known Rossi Lemeni, the tenors Galliano Masini, Max Lorenz, Infantino, Scattolini, Mafalda Favero, Cloe Elmo and the Konetzni sisters from the Vienna Opera. Sergio Failloni and Georges Sebastian were the conductors. The company was due to be launched in January of 1947 in Chicago and then take on an important tour. Naturally, Bagarotzy put Callas in the cast as they had secretly started having an affair. According to his plans, Callas was to sing the lead in the inaugural production of Turandot conducted by Failloni, who together with Galliano Masini and Mafalda Favero was expecting a well-known singer for the role.

Knowing that the maestro and his wife needed help in their home in New York and particularly for little Donatella their daughter, Bagarotzy arranged to have Maria taken into their service at once. After about two months Maria plucked up enough courage to ask Failloni for an audition. He was quite taken aback but agreed to listen to her. After hearing her in "Casta Diva" he decided to help her, finding her amazingly talented and her voice ready. The first thing he did was to accept her into the cast of *Turandot*. The rehearsals started in New York and in early January continued in Chicago. According to the advance publicity, the opera was due to open on January 6 at the Civic Opera but due to a dispute with the already powerful artists union over a deposit of funds that the company was unable to make guaranteeing the payment of the chorus, the opera was postponed until January 27, and then, after being declared bankrupt, was cancelled along with the tour. The artists who had traveled from Europe had to find last minute concerts and otherwise improvise to pay their way home again. Maria, having lost her one chance and finding herself once again without work and very unhappy, made ends meet by singing at the Asti restaurant in the Village where the singing was by and large performed by gifted amateurs and professionals of modest talent, in an atmosphere of cheerfulness and where she at least had an audience.

The fact that she sang there is confirmed by the well-known journalist and author Ilario Fiore who, before returning to live in Rome, had been the correspondent of the RAI (Italian radio and television network) in New York for many years. Here is his story:

> I think that many people forget that Maria Callas was born an American, in New York, to a family of Greek immigrants.
>
> Only a stone's throw from their home there was – and still is – a restaurant called "Asti" well known to opera lovers.
>
> Their specialty is not the Bagnacauda with sweet cardi or the fondue with white truffles but the charming idea to have Bel Canto waiters who serve the customers while singing arias from their favorite operas. I did not frequent the restaurant because of the singing, but because I am from the town of Asti in Italy and I would go there to visit a good friend of mine, Ugo Bigliani, also from Asti who worked there as a waiter. He has a wonderful bass voice and now lives in Flushing Meadows where every year on the first Sunday in

October we would celebrate the feast of The Madonna of the rosary with some serious drinking.

It was in the winter of 1946-47 that a twenty-three year old Greek-American girl went to work there, more for the singing than for the money. She had left New York at age fourteen to study at the conservatory in Athens. Her favorites were "La Gioconda" and "Norma" and her "Suicidio" and "Casta Diva" arias were an immediate hit. It was here that she met Nicola Rossi Lemeni who was then singing at the Metropolitan.

The meeting with Failloni had not been in vain. After having conducted *Aida* and *La Traviata* in the 1946 season at the Arena the previous year, he had been offered the direction of the inaugural opera of the 1947 season *La Gioconda*.

He accepted and wrote a letter to the famous tenor of the Metropolitan Opera Giovanni Zenatello, who was also artistic director of the Arena putting forward Maria's name for the role and asking for an audition. Rossi Lemeni who had been engaged to sing at the Arena in Faust also recommended his friend Maria highly. At this point all they could do was await Zenatello's decision.

Zenatello was the first person to realize the possibilities of using the Arena of Verona for Opera and sang in the first *Aida* in the Arena in 1913. His daughter Nina tells of her father's meeting with Callas:

> In late April of 1947, Zenatello was in New York and had planned to return to Verona within a few months to take care of the final preparations for the annual season of Opera that took place in the Arena of Verona in July and August. In his periods of absence from Verona he had left all his work in the capable hands of his cousin and opera buff, Gaetano Pomari.
>
> Immediately on arriving in New York, Zenatello set to work seeing agents, seeing impresarios, the management of the Metropolitan, musicians and friends but first and foremost, he trusted the judgment of his friend Toscanini who had him listen to on of his protégées, the soprano Herva Nelli, whom he thought would be excellent for the Arena in *Gioconda*.
>
> Zenatello listened to her and liked what he heard but was not over-enthusiastic. He decided to wait a few weeks before making a decision.
>
> Meanwhile his search did not stop. A friend of his, Bagarotzy the lawyer, who had married a singer and to please his wife had also become an impresario,

asked him to delay his decision until he had heard a new voice that he was sure would be of interest to him.

One day that spring, two young ladies arrived at the Zenatello home at 50 Central Park West for the audition. One of them, Louise Caselotti was attractive and elegantly dressed, the other, quite the opposite even though she had done her best. This did not matter as Zenatello was interested only in the voices. The other girl was Maria Callas and was just twenty-four years old. Caselotti sang first a mezzo-soprano piece accompanied by Callas and it was not the voice of the mezzo that impressed Zenatello, a true delusion for him, but the masterful way that Callas had accompanied her. The first point in her favor was her consummate musicality. Callas then sang "Casta Diva" from *Norma* with Caselotti at the piano. She sang it with such mastery that at the end of the audition Zenatello, who was swept up with enthusiasm applauded and embraced her. It wasn't the beauty and size of her voice that impressed him but the artistic ability as interpreter that she displayed with such natural spontaneity, rare understanding and lively intelligence. He immediately decided to give her lessons and discover her full ability and repair a few obvious defects in a torrential voice that was sometimes out of control. Fully understanding all the problems and trials of a young singer (having experienced them himself) and being convinced of her potential, one evening he said to his daughter: "I can assure you that that young girl's troubles are over. She will have the career she deserves. It's not for nothing that I'm the director of the Arena of Verona and it's from there that I'll make her famous in the whole world. Wait and see."

Zenatello signed her for the lead in *Gioconda* instead of Toscanini's protégée and gave Callas her debut in the Arena.

Callas returned to Zenatello for lessons every afternoon for the two months remaining before their departure. He had discovered a small defect in her middle register and insisted on working on it as often as possible. The time available was not enough and Callas retained this tiny defect forever. Meanwhile, Zenatello, who had not accepted a penny for the lessons, informed his cousin Pomari in Verona all about the "Perla nera" (Black pearl) he had discovered and had contracted for Gioconda. He was instructed to tell the press, assuring them that in the summer they would be able to hear a truly exceptional voice. Pomari didn't need to be told twice. Word reached the ears of a mutual friend, Battista Meneghini, who, the previous year had, together with Zenatello, searched in vain for the right voice. On hearing that Giovanni had found an extraordinary singer in America Meneghini became interested in her before even meeting her saying that if Zenatello had chosen her she must certainly be exceptional. Callas' destiny had been decided: from her first day in Verona, Meneghini was at her side, the rest is history.

Having discovered an exceptional talent for the soprano lead in Gioconda he now needed a tenor who was of the same level of beauty for vocal interpretation. Richard Tucker was signed. This tenor, though at the beginning of his career, had been singing for a while at the Metropolitan but was relatively unknown in Italy. Tucker, with his beautiful dramatic tenor voice, would be another revelation of the fortunate season at the Arena. Elena Nicolai and the baritone Tagliabue sang the other principal roles.

Other great artists that season were: Renata Tebaldi and Rossi Lemeni in *Faust* and the tenor Picchi, Adriana Guerrini, Nicolai and Tagliabue who were performing in *Un Ballo in Maschera*.

When all was ready, and he had booked the tickets, hoping to have some well-deserved rest after his American activities, he got ill. His doctors forbade him to travel and ordered him total rest for two months. He retired to the country where the climate was better than the chaos of both New York and Verona.

Zenatello, with bitterness in his big heart, had to resign himself to the fact that he would not be able put the finishing touches to what would be his penultimate season at the Arena and be present to take pleasure in the triumph of his new discovery. Undoubtedly Bagarotzy, along with Failloni and Rossi Lemeni, played a part in Callas getting a contract with the Arena. Shrewdly, Bagarotzy had convinced Callas to sign a contract with him for ten percent of this and all future earnings. Maria signed more than likely out of a feeling of gratitude and the fact that they were emotionally involved. Louise Caselotti went with her in order to collect the fees and also try to sing auditions.

In the meantime Callas had met Meneghini who offered her protection and friendship. Maria, from Verona, continued her correspondence with Bagarotzy telling him about a "wonderful person" that she had met and asked his advice on her decisions writing with a confidentiality that would indicate that their relationship had been intimate.

These letters dated, August 20, September 2, and October 25, 1947, would prove to be extremely costly to Callas.

She had signed the contract with him on June 13, 1947, three days before signing for the Arena. Richard Bagarotzy waited for seven years before presenting her with the bill for his percentage. The sum, an incredible amount in those days was for three hundred thousand dollars. The moment he chose was the great diva's return to America for her performances of *Norma, Traviata* and *Lucia* in Chicago. After the final performance Callas found herself backstage surrounded by the sheriffs. According to American law for a writ to be valid it has to be served by touching the party concerned. Callas, once realizing what was going on started to scream and tried to get out of the clutches of the men. There is a famous photograph of the event with Callas, eyes glaring and mouth wide open. The artist Molino published a beautiful drawing of this scene on the cover of the newspaper Domenica del Corriere as the event of the week. Meneghini hired lawyers in Italy and in the United States and Maria wrote an explanation of how the contract had been coerced and for that reason was extortion. Nelly Failloni, the wife of the conductor, who had meanwhile taken on the job of impresario for the Hungarian State Opera, proved a valuable defense witness when in 1956 she wrote her version of the facts.

Callas wrote to her from her home in Via Buonarotti in Milan asking her to bear witness:

Dear Nelly,

I am troubling you for a favor from the soul, the soul I know so well.

As you know, I am in litigation with Bagarotzy who is making the most insane demands among which are the following two:

First – that I had been created and taught by his wife and that he had spent not less than $85,000 dollars to enable me to sing.

Second – that he had expressly mounted the Chicago season for me; and you know how that ended.

I therefore need a letter from you stating all the facts regarding Bagarotzy that you know as you lived through them with that unforgettable maestro – your husband.

I leave for America in fifteen days and hope to have news from you.

Kindest regards to Donatella and kiss her for me. (Donatella, the little girl that Callas had been baby-sitter to had become a noted pianist.)

My husband joins me in sending our kindest and most affectionate greetings

Yours ever
Maria

Nelly Failloni answered immediately with a long and detailed account that was useful in setting out the facts. The situation was improving for Callas and the lawyers were feeling optimistic when the perfidious Bagarotzy sent copies of Maria's letters to Meneghini via his lawyers threatening to include them in the evidence and make them public. It would have been devastating for the public image of Maria. In one of the letters Maria writes:

> Out of sight, out of mind. I refuse to believe this old saying and I beg you not to believe it either. I think you are bright enough to understand more than what I am writing . . .

At the end of the letter she writes:

> I am as bad as you, don't be selfish and don't misunderstand me: I still feel the same about you as when I left. Well, I end this long letter with a kiss on both your cheeks and . . . maybe one on your tempting mouth . . .

All Meneghini could do was to arrive at a compromise and ended up paying a fortune to end the legal proceedings. Nelly Failloni replied and at length confirmed that Callas had worked for the family in New York, in 1946-47, helping with the housework and looking after the baby Donatella. This has all been recounted in an interview recently published on CD by La Scala and also to journalists from leading Italian publications, Carla Pilolli of the *Messaggiero,* Matilde Amorosi of *Gente* and Roberto Tumbarello of *Oggi.*

On the occasion of the Callas exhibition in Venice, Donatella Failloni reconfirmed in a televised interview with Simonetta Simoni the fact that Callas had been her babysitter. Jackie, Callas' sister, who today lives in Athens with her younger husband, feels that these allegations are unfounded and only based on her word (she was not with her in America in 1947), while an entire dossier of letters between Callas and the Failloni family exists. Maria never forgot all they did for her and remained close to Nelly all her life. In September of 1977 Nelly called from Budapest begging her desperately to join her in the Hungarian capital; she never arrived. Instead, she received a phone call from Maria's maid saying that the Signora was dead.

Let us now return to *Gioconda* and the review from the newspaper *L'Arena* of August 3 and written by G. Bertolaso.

> Two voices reigned supreme in this production of *Gioconda,* voices from America and as such unknown, that shone forth from the radiant interpreters Maria Callas and Richard Tucker. Callas, the soprano, was a protagonist of class, passionate, rich in tone particularly in the high register where the notes were effortless and vibrant. As an actress, she gave her role all the precision and vigor needed in both the part that required emotion and above all the more dramatic parts where she sang without sparing her remarkable vocal resources. Her success culminated with the great aria Suicidio in the second part of the fourth act.

The same newspaper had published a sort of portrait interview with the newest star of the Arena on July 30. It was not entirely true that even though her first operatic endeavors had recognizable defects, she had not gone unobserved.

Let us leave it to the journalist from *L'Arena* to give us an account, this too only recently discovered and most enjoyable for its ardent style:

> All singers of note have moments in their lives that they cherish above all others. They tell of their first acknowledgements in the theater improvised by their families and friends, or in the solemnity of a church decorated for a feast day. The relatives become the audience; the friends represent the great public of tomorrow and together they become the critics, admirers, and fans. At times the career of a celebrated artist is born in those little theatres where there is no money and are no ushers with gilded buttons.
>
> Maria Callas, the central character of Ponchielli's masterpiece *La Gioconda* which opens on Saturday in the Arena, is one of these singers and is bound with unwavering passion to her memories. It was her family that discovered her voice; she was a vivacious and graceful child with a sweet and strong voice that rang out in the upper register like a nightingale in the season of love calling out in the mysterious peace of the forest. In love with music, she studied the piano with brilliant results; at eleven years of age she won a singing competition with her impressive and brilliant qualities; the first prize was a gold watch that she still treasures today.

And again:

> Maria Callas is a sweet and sensitive person. She is in love with Italy, its cities, and its villages that are dotted among lakes and seas like the beads of magic rosaries and its people, smiling and amiable.
>
> She believed that Italy was still suffering the nightmare of the unspeakable atrocities that had befallen her during the appalling misadventure of the war; instead she has found a hard working hive of activity and ideas. This American singer is particularly taken with our city.
>
> She has been conquered – that is the correct word – by the exceptional Scaligeran attractions of our city. When she is not rehearsing in the Arena she enjoys wandering through the city's quiet streets, its most secret and evocative corners and its ancient churches. Maria Callas, who speaks with a soft and languid voice took her leave from us expressing once again her appreciation for our city and that she would be happy to live in Italy forever.

Callas' success in the early stages of her career is largely due to the help she received from Ferruccio Cusinati (1872 – 1954), the highly respected chorus master of both the Arena and the Fenice in Venice and teacher at the conservatory. As a friend of Serafin and Meneghini, he accepted the position of being Callas' teacher. If De Hidalgo taught Callas the technique of singing, Cusinati, a refined connoisseur of voices, prepared Callas' entire repertoire in the early years of her Italian career starting with *Gioconda*.

At the end of rehearsals in the Arena, Callas would run to Via Valverde and would study for hours with dedication and passion. She learned exceptionally quickly and managed to correct some of her faults in time for the *Gioconda* and, thanks to the experience of her colleague, became very well prepared for the role.

We received a remarkable testimonial from Cusinati's daughter Isolda, which was clear and coherent even though she had turned ninety-four years old.

> Callas' husband had entrusted her to my father just a few days after her arrival in Verona to put the finishing touches to her voice for Gioconda before the rehearsals started.

Cusinati said, even though recognizing her exceptional talent, "She will have to start all over again, right from the scales." She had glaring defects and her voice had a wobble. For *Gioconda*, the low register was good but the upper register, even though strong, was annoyingly shrill. Even Serafin had defined Callas' voice as a *meravigliosa vociaccia* (magnificent ugly voice). The wavering was most noticeable in the high notes. "It sounds like a ship coming into port," Cusinati said, comparing it to a siren. She was however very intelligent and extraordinarily musical. No miracles could be worked for *Gioconda* but the results were long lasting.

Later, Meneghini put pressure on my father saying, "Maestro Cusinati, let's get it all done quickly, let her go out and sing because I can't get her out from under my feet." Cusinati taught her all the operas in the early years, *Medea* being learned in only eight days.

Maria quite rightly said, "After me, no one will be able to sing this opera." And then about her ascendancy with the public: "One does not always need to exist, you only need to make believe, to exist."

After her debut in the Arena, Cusinati prepared Maria for her Scala audition with Maestro Labroca, then the artistic director of La Scala (presented by Antonio Guarnieri) but the result was negative even though she had sung *Casta Diva* very well. In January of 1950 she sang *Aida* at the Teatro Grande in Brescia. In the beginning Cusinati tried to dissuade her from accepting as he thought it too premature but after an uncertain start the outcome was more than adequate, for Callas' level that is.

There is a charming dedication to Cusinati from Callas: *To my very dear Maestro Cusinati – who suffered greatly in preparing Tristan with me. With infinite respect. Maria Callas.* This opera by Wagner was performed in Venice at the Fenice on November 30 and was the second opera for Callas in Italy.

Knowing how sparing she was with praise one must assume that Callas had the utmost respect for the maestro. One of the first people Maria Callas met in Verona was Giorgio Alzanese, a boy of fifteen who was of Greek origin. The meeting took place on stage while her substitute was rehearsing, the boy made a negative comment in Greek and Callas, overhearing, nodded, happy to find a compatriot in Verona. Alzanese became her interpreter as she had only been in Italy a few days and did not speak Italian correctly yet. Alzanese recalls:

> I remember that Callas was lodged at the Hotel Accademia in Via Leoncino near San Fermo, she would often eat at the Pedavena restaurant as

Meneghini's guest but more often as the guest of Gaetano Pomari, the proprietor. He was a cousin of Zenatello and his right hand man at the Arena. Callas also wrote a dedication to him writing: *To my dear Gaetano, only you know how much I owe you.*

Maria, who enjoyed my mother's cooking very much was very fond of her and called her Madam Mary. Her favorite dish was meatballs, the classic Greek dish with the meat ground very fine, lots of onions and with bread soaked in milk to make them softer and then again, those stewed in tomatoes with strong spices. Tomatoes, zucchini and vine leaves stuffed with rice.

She was simple, never wore any make-up. She dressed modestly and always slightly comically. She was a bit primitive, a big girl but always natural and amusing. I remember always how beautifully she did her hair when I accompanied her to have her first photograph taken at the photographer Tommasoli in piazza San Niccolo. Maria always had a good appetite; at this point she wasn't too fat yet, but put on a lot of weight in the next few years. We would buy sandwiches filled with Bondola that she loved so much from the Simonetti salami shop near the Marconi cinema and would then go with our bags full of food to the Pedavena and have our lunch. Some might not believe it, but often Maria would send me to buy Serraglio cigarettes and after lunch would enjoy a smoke. When she had learned Italian she realized that by listening to others, she had instead learned Veronese.

Immediately after Verona, the second city that launched her career and that caught her imagination was Venice. She arrived in the city in the summer of 1947 and with Meneghini explored the quaint streets and visited all the best-known sights. She was enraptured by the Titian "Assumption" in the Frari Basilica and would often ask to taken back just so she could pay a brief visit to her "Madonna."

It was on the stage of the Fenice and later that of the Comunale in Florence that we would see Callas launched on a secure path to fame. This review by Giuseppe Pugliese, critic writing for *Il Gazettino* discusses her debut in *Tristan and Isolde* on January 30, 1948:

> An artist of unusual perception, sure and blessed in the art of acting, laid bare the ardent passions of the role with sweetness and feminine ardor rather than virility and solemnity, where her beautiful warm voice, brilliant in the upper register, found ringing emphasis and appropriate lyricism.

A few days later on the same stage in a role no less demanding but of a different style and difficulty she sang Puccini's Turandot. Again Pugliese penned her praises:

> *Turandot* was admirable for the incisive brilliance of her voice most effective in the upper register, her exquisite sensitivity and her extraordinary intelligence on stage makes one forget the occasional fluctuation of timbre in the voice; she confronted the daunting extension of the role with energy and security shaping it with emphasis or pureness according to the requirements of the part.

On the subject of her miracle in *I Puritani* that we have already dealt with at some length, Pugliese wrote the following:

> In the abrupt passage from one opera to the other (referring to the recent performance of *The Valkyrie*), most other singers with the voice and temperament of Callas but not her intelligence would have failed. Not Callas. Being the great singer that she is and by varying the vocal and scenic exigency of the role, she enjoyed moments of authentic artistry and having overcome the technicalities of trills, scales and embellishments, gave an interpretation of great musical intensity from the more lyric moments to the vertiginous heights of the drama. In short, an interpretation worthy of all the role requires.

After her debut in *Tristan* Callas sang in Venice until 1954.

Callas made her La Scala debut on April 12, 1950 substituting for an indisposed Renata Tebaldi in *Aida* with Mario del Monaco and Fedora Barbieri. Giringhelli (the general manager at the time) ignored her and did not pay the customary visit to her dressing room. The critics were also decidedly cold. All this changed soon with the direct and impassioned interest of Arturo Toscanini. It was Luigi Stefanotti, a businessman from Parma, an opera lover and ardent admirer of Callas who persistently told Toscanini about her. He was one of the privileged few who were regular guests in the Toscanini home.

Toscanini, who at that time was eighty-three years old and in precarious health (he died seven years later), was not only interested in La Scala but in all that went on in the other theaters as well as in the provinces particularly whenever any interesting new talented young singers were to be found.

Toscanini had been receiving notices from all quarters (not only Stefanotti) of Callas being someone to watch. He knew about the *Norma* in Florence, the *Parsifal* in Rome and the tours in Argentina and Mexico.

Callas had not yet sung *Macbeth* and Toscanini knew that she had received an invitation to sing in the Maggio Musicale in Florence in 1951, the year that he had planned to do a big production of *Macbeth* in the September to commemorate the fiftieth anniversary of Verdi's death. At the insistence of Stefanotti, Wally Toscanini approached Callas and invited her to sing for the maestro at his home in Via Diurni on September 27, 1950. Finding herself in front of the great Maestro, for the first time in her life, Callas was unusually nervous. Toscanini put her at her ease and after lunch, without further ado told her that he wanted to conduct *Macbeth* and had not been able to find the right singer in Europe or the U.S.A for the soprano role. "She should be an ugly woman, evil, with a bitter voice, suffocating and dark," he said. Even though she was sight-reading the part, Callas showed great determination and almost instinctively expressed what he was looking for, not only doing what he asked but also displaying her astonishing voice. After reading through the first act, Toscanini closed the score and said, "Thank you, you will sing *Macbeth* with me. Tomorrow I will call Giringhelli and tell him to get the Scala *Macbeth* at Busseto with Toscanini operation underway." Giringhelli called but unfortunately the *Macbeth* never took place. Callas waited till the last minute to sign with Florence considering that Toscanini had naturally asked her for exclusivity but the Comunale was no longer considering Macbeth but had decided on Rossini's *Armida*.

Her positive impression on Toscanini proved to be of great help in America as well as opening the doors to La Scala. While he had been working from New York on getting Scala to do the *Macbeth* in Busseto, Toscanini had been talking continually about Callas and shortly afterwards Rudolf Bing, the general manager of the Metropolitan Opera, expressed his interest.

Toscanini asked Callas to accept the invitation of a young composer Giancarlo Menotti to sing in his opera *The Consul* at La Scala but, after having looked at the score she refused. She did not feel that she could play a contemporary role. Callas had several other unforgettable meetings with Toscanini, after his last concert in Milan on September 19, 1952 and again at the end of November in 1954 while she was rehearsing *La Vestale* with Visconti and Votto. There is a beautiful photograph of Callas, Toscanini, Votto and Visconti in the deserted orchestra of the theater. Her last meeting with the Maestro was once again in the darkened stalls of La Scala during a rehearsal of *Carmen* conducted by Von Karajan. It was January of 1955 and Toscanini not being fond of *Carmen* only whispered a few words to Maria and, without saying anything more, left with an indifferent expression on his face. Callas sang *Macbeth* at La Scala in 1952 conducted by De Sabata.

The first person to know about Callas' meeting with Toscanini was Elvira De Hidalgo. On October 11, 1950 from Rome where she was singing *Aida,* Maria wrote:

> Only a few lines to send my love and tell you some great news. I have been chosen by Toscanini to sing Lady Macbeth. After having sung for him he decided to do it for the Verdi commemoration in September 1951.

Toscanini's esteem was a source of great pride for Maria who would describe to her friends over and over again about the day she first met him in the house in Via Diurni.

When Wally showed her into the salon she was immediately struck by a fine portrait of the Maestro, well lit and framed above the fireplace. She remained observing it for a long time and when the Maestro arrived for the audition, tired but still with the famous sharp twinkle in his eye, found the likeness remarkable. She thought that once she was famous she too would like a portrait painted by the same artist.

This artist was Stefano Caselli, Florentine through and through, and though still very young, already known and greatly admired in the salons of Milan. His drawings and paintings of famous people in the art and music world, Richard Strauss, Stravinski, Thomas Mann and Benedetto Croce among others, were well known. In 1957 Maria had her wish granted and this was the only time she ever sat for an artist. All other portraits of Callas, though good likenesses, were done from photographs after her death. Maria sat for Caselli for days and days.

The preparatory drawings and photographs of the sittings still exist but unfortunately the portrait was destroyed in the terrible fire that destroyed the Fenice Theater in Venice in January 1996. Caselli has painted another with the same figure of Callas and has inserted the burning theater into the background. The absolute talent and greatness of Callas have enabled her legend to live beyond the flames and the new painting by Caselli has set her terrestrial likeness through her powerful gaze.

Promoted by Totaro Wajima of the Voice Factory, a contributor to the rebuilding of the Venetian theater, the new work, painted using a multimedia technique and the splendid serigraphy, was inaugurated on the occasion of the Callas exhibition in Tokyo. Significantly it coincided with the fiftieth anniversary of Callas' debut in *Tristan and Isolde* at the Fenice.

We close our story of the early years of Callas' career with her opening of the 1954 season at La Scala with *La Vestale* directed by Visconti.

La Domenica del Corriere, the most popular weekly magazine at the time, dedicated the cover to her. Maria was the Queen of Milan. The Martini and Rossi concerts, famous music sponsors of the day, the operas broadcast live and her first recordings were a great help in promoting the popularity of Callas.

The CETRA recording company, well known for contracting young singers who had not yet reached celebrity status is fortunate to include a number of recordings by Maria Meneghini-Callas in their archives before she was a star and more than just an up and coming artist.

Thanks to this Turin Company, the avid record collectors can own recordings of Callas and hear her voice at the beginning of her career, a voice that she gradually refined and stylized and here can be heard in its full glory, revelling in the entire range of sounds without risking homogeneity and depth. It is also true however that the timbre was still quite immature in some areas and seemed less supple in the passaggio. At that time we were treated to the double surprise of what a voice like hers was capable of in two totally different operas: *Gioconda* and *Traviata*. In both of these operas she displayed enormous dramatic and vocal power. Even in the more somber moments, Callas was able to bring the character to life with total vocal and artistic domination.

Actually having three voices at her disposal (even in Verdi's time it was considered a necessity to interpret *Traviata*), Callas has left a record of a complete Violetta. Supple in the vocal line and with freedom of agility in the phrasing in this work by Verdi, Callas achieved the full artistic circle with her interpretation of this role.

It is unlikely that we will ever again be able to find a voice like that of Maria Meneghini Callas.

Her meeting with Walter Legge and his illustrious consort the great Elisabeth Schwarzkopf led to her signing an exclusive contract with Columbia (now EMI). After having heard the first recordings done with CETRA and having been, in his own words, astounded, Legge wanted his wife with him when he made the big decision. They heard her in *Traviata* in Parma on December 29 1951. Schwarzkopf recalls:

> At the time she was robust and prosperous, nothing like the delicate and fragile Violetta of La Scala. Maria sang wonderfully, her voice brimmed over with sound, I remember only one high note being slightly veiled. She received the triumph she deserved. As you know there is no triumph in Italy as important and gratifying as the approval of a Verdi role in Parma. From that day on, whenever possible, I never missed an opera or concert with Maria. Unfortunately I was not able to attend the Tosca recording with De Sabata, but I'll never forget the Visconti and Karajan Lucia di Lammermoor in Vienna. Having screamed Brava every time she made a curtain call, I arrived in her dressing room with no voice at all.
>
> It was with Lucia, recorded in Florence at the Maggio Musicale of 1953 with Gobbi and Di Stefano that Callas started her lifelong recording career with EMI.

THE VOICE OF THE YOUNG CALLAS

Mario Merigo

The appearance of Maria Callas on the Italian stage in 1947 was a unique and astonishing event, an event that changed the way we view the soprano and mezzo soprano voice.

From time immemorial we had not heard a soprano capable of singing the light repertoire with such incisive accent and giving a new dignity to the art of florid singing. More than this, it gave back to the early Verdi works all the technique and interpretation we had thought lost forever. Her work in Greece, as well as her early Italian performances, are lost to us as there are no known recordings of these operas. The earliest recordings we have were made in 1949 and they give us Callas the phenomenon in all its explosive newness. *Elvira* in *I Puritani*, *Isolde*, *Norma*, *Turandot*.

Without a doubt her voice was exceptional. Her timbre was not of the highest quality, the color, dark and metallic, the voice was capable of great extension in the upper register but with the center and lower register strongly constructed and rather guttural. This fact allowed easy imitation of her voice but not the stature of her interpretations.

Today we still marvel at how, thanks to her repertoire, incredibly diverse repertoires can coexist: Wagner and Rossini, pure Belcanto and the eloquence of the Verismo school. It was Elvira De Hidalgo who created the voice of Maria Callas with years of study in Greece. Maria remained in affectionate correspondence with De Hidalgo who, in a letter dated 1949 writes: "While the others told you at sixteen years of age that you were a dramatic soprano, I made you sing *Cenerentola* and do all the scales of a light soprano: That is why today you can astound everyone singing *I Puritani* and *Parsifal*." De Hidalgo, who had been a noted light soprano at the turn of the century, understood that behind the dark timbre of Maria's voice there was great potential for agility that absolutely had to be nurtured. Callas herself remembered the precious lessons learned from her Spanish teacher to always "keep the voice light," to never put weight on the voice, particularly in the coloratura repertoire. Thanks to an excellent vocal placement her voice was penetrating and incisive: this allowed the renaissance of the mythical so-called "dramatic coloratura" sopranos like Pasta and Malibran before there was a distinction between the repertoires of the light and the dramatic sopranos.

De Hidalgo was like a mother to Callas. Her relationship with her own mother was difficult and problematic. She was forced by her mother into singing at an early age and became a sort of *enfant prodige*, not to be loved but exhibited in public. Once Callas had become famous, her mother continually asked her for money. The teacher/pupil relationship with De Hidalgo, on the other hand, developed into a forty-year long friendship, filled with support and shared intimacy. The years of correspondence with her teacher who had been her mentor since adolescence in Greece during the last years of the war make this evident. She always acknowledged the fact that it was De Hidalgo who had sweetened her voice, a voice filled with youthful, excessive resentment.

Strictly from a vocal point of view, Callas, who was to experience an unstoppable rise to fame, was at her best in the early years prior to her fast and early decline. Unfortunately, this greatness is most often only available on live recordings which are not always of the best quality.

One can hear Callas in an extraordinary complete recording of *Nabucco* conducted by Vittorio Gui performed in Naples in 1949. Here she is in wonderful voice and presents us with a biting and effective interpretation of Abigaille. However what is most striking is the intensity of the interpretation: Callas, right from the first notes, appears to be blessed with a rigorous and logical capacity to analyze. Nevertheless her interpretation does not start with the text in a philological sense but from a new reading of the tradition in terms of vocal faculty. This is even more noticeable in the works of Donizetti and Bellini. Her *Puritani*, her *Lucia di Lammermoor* or her *Norma*, as far as cuts and cadenzas go, did not present particular innovation: nor could they with conductors like Serafin, Votto and Gui. Callas' revolution on one hand was due to her voice, thanks to the awareness that coloratura is a dramatic vehicle, and on the other, with an interpretation considered "reformed." We only have to think of *Norma*, transformed by previous singers into a Priestess virago and reformed to her melodramatic dignity by Maria Callas. This revolution/restoration (these innovations were taken from the methods used in the theaters at the beginning of the nineteenth century as used by Malibran and Pasta) was the initial cause for misunderstandings on behalf of some critics and musical associations.

This did not stop Callas from quickly becoming a living legend. The only complete Wagnerian opera available with Callas is *Parsifal,* in Italian, under the direction of Vittorio Gui in 1950. Her Kundry is one of admirable measure and balance, intense and expressive with all the voice required.

That voice was to remain intact for only a few years in the early 1950s. One can take for example her *Traviata*. Comparing the Scala Production in 1955, quite justifiably celebrated, Callas seems in better form in the 1952 recording from Mexico with Giuseppe Di Stefano and the CETRA recording with Francesco Albanese. In contrast to her male colleagues, Callas was alarmingly superior. The technique is excellent but what shines through is her ability to phrase, to capture previously unrecognized details in the conversational parts of the singing. All this happened before she met Luchino Visconti. Callas was to have sung *Macbeth* with Toscanini in 1951 in Busseto for the Verdi celebrations. Her audition with the great conductor in 1950 was definitely one of the most significant events in the life of the young soprano. As is well known, this project never came to fruition. But in 1952 at La Scala under the direction of Victor De Sabata, Callas was able to perform an extraordinary *Lady Macbeth*, which was to be recognized as fundamental to the history of interpretation. From the recording we can hear the dark and mysterious accents of the character, a superb elasticity in her voice and the magnificent capacity to dominate the lower register of the role.

Her contribution to the interpretation of *Lucia di Lammermoor* is also of major importance. Successive singers might have sung with more purity and levity, but Callas, with her full and dark timbre, with her dramatic coloratura, put all the light sopranos, from the second half of the nineteenth century onwards, into the shade. Doing this, she revitalized a type of voice, the dramatic coloratura soprano favored in the period of Donizetti.

Predating the recordings in 1954 (Columbia) and in 1955 (Karajan at La Scala) we can hear the mad scenes in Mexico City. In 1952 Callas was making her Mexican debut in one of her best known roles. In February of the same year she had performed the mad scene in a concert recorded by the RAI. Of the three performances, the 10th, the 14th and the 26th of

June, we can listen to four mad scenes. At the premier, after twenty minutes of applause, Callas was obliged to repeat the entire scene. Over and above her splendid vocal form, we can hear in the nobility of her singing the makings of the great singer-actress who would blossom in the years to come, even when her vocal abilities had abandoned her.

AFTERWORD

Francesca Valente

It was 1958 when Maria Callas performed for the first time in California in an extraordinary concert at the Shrine Auditorium in Los Angeles. Over fifty years after the memorable encounter of La Divina with the City of Angels, I have decided to pay a tribute to the greatest opera singer of the twentieth century by staging the exhibition *Maria Callas: a Woman, a Voice, a Myth,* and by publishing this book with the support of all the Italian Cultural Institutes in the United States. *The Young Maria Callas* includes a rare and revealing diary written by Callas herself about the seminal Italian years which changed her life. This publication maps a journey from her unhappy childhood as a child prodigy to a real turning point in her career with an historical performance as Norma at the Maggio Musicale Fiorentino. She then started singing in the most celebrated Italian theatres, from Teatro Comunale in Florence to San Carlo in Naples, from Rome Opera to La Scala in Milan, under the baton of many distinguished conductors, including Tullio Serafin, Erich Kleiber, Leonard Bernstein and Arturo Toscanini. Her first performance at La Fenice, Venice in 1947 deserves a special mention; it was in *Tristan and Isolde* by Richard Wagner, the composer whose music, more than anybody else's, enhanced her extraordinary skills.

She combined indeed an impressive *bel canto* technique with great dramatic gifts. An extremely versatile singer, her repertoire ranged from classical *opera seria* to the *bel canto* operas of Donizetti, Bellini, and Rossini which she revisited with an entirely new approach. Called by Leonard Bernstein the "The Bible of opera," her influence is so enduring that the City of Venice named a bridge and a walkway leading to the old La Fenice gate and the new Aldo Rossi hall, after her. Moreover the City will soon inaugurate a museum presenting the diva's memorabilia, stage costumes, rare documents, jewels, books, letters and archival photographs collected over years of research with passionate love by Bruno Tosi.

A first exhibition of this kind went on display in 1993 at the Olivetti Showroom designed by Carlo Scarpa in Venice, and then toured the world from Paris to New York, from Athens to Tokyo, from Rome to Los Angeles, receiving huge applause from both public and critics.

We like to think that the great unforgettable soprano, praised by poets and artists such as Pier Paolo Pasolini and Enzo Cucchi, belongs to Italy as our country gradually transformed her from a shy, insecure Greek American girl, born in New York, to a groundbreaking artist and a sophisticated diva under the magic wand of the legendary director Luchino Visconti. The truth is that Maria Callas doesn't belong to the United States, Greece or Italy, but to the entire world. Her legacy is universal.

CHRONOLOGY

1923
December 2: Maria Anna Sophie Cecilia Kalogeropoulos is born in New York. Her parents, George and Evangelia Kalogeropoulos had emigrated froom Greece to Long Island, New York in August 1923.

1929
George Kalogeropoulos sets up a pharmachy in a Greek quarter of Manhattan and changes the family name to Callas.

1932
Maria is given her fist paino lessons. Later in life she is able to study all her roles at the piano without the help of a *repetiteur.*

1937
The Callas parents separate. Evangelia returns to Greece with her two daughters and changes the family name back to Kalogeropoulos.

1938
Maria Kalogeropoulos is admitted to the National Conservatoire in Athens despite being younger than the minimun age requirement of 16, and begins her studies under Maria Trivella.
April 11: Appears with fellow students in first pubblic recital.

1939
April 2: Maria makes her stage debut as Santuzza in a student production of *Cavalleria Rusticana* and wins the Conservatoire's prize. Elvira de Hidalgo becomes Maria's teacher at the Conservatoire and concentrates on coloratura training.

1940
October 21: First engagement with the Lyric Theatre company, singing songs in Shakespeare's *Merchant of Venice* at the Royal Theatre in Athens.

1941

January 21: Makes her professional operatic debut as Beatrice in *Boccaccio* at the Palas Cinema with the Lyric Theatre company with whom she will sing in *Tosca, Tiefland, Cavalleria Rusticana, Fidelio,* and *Der Bettelstudent* during the next four years.

1942

August 27: Sings *Tosca* for the first time in Greek at an open-air performance at the Park Summer Theatre Kaftmonos Square.

1944

The occupying forces lose control over Greece and the British fleet arrives in Piraeus. Maria Kalogeropoulos decides to returns to the U.S.A. and find her father.

1945

August 3: Gives a farewell concert in Athens, her first solo recital, to raise money for her journey to the USA. September Returns to New York and takes up the name of Callas again. December : Auditions for the Metropolitan Opera, but fails to secure an engagement.

1946

Tries unsuccessfully to find work, but continues strenuous vocal pratice to perfect her technique. Meets agent Eddie Bagarozy. Accepts engagement to sing in Turandot in Chicago in January 1947 with a cast of celebrated European singers in a new company to be founded by Bagarozy and Ottavio Scotto, an Italian impresario.

1947

January: The Chicago company goes bankrupt a few days before its scheduled opening performance. Nicola Rossi Lemeni, the Italian bass, is also a member of the company and introduces Callas to Giovanni Zanatello, who is in the U.S.A. to find singers for the 1947 Verona Opera Festival of which he is the Artistic Director. He engages Callas to sing in *La Gioconda.*
June 27: Callas arrives in Naples and goes the next day to Verona to begin rehearsals for *La Gioconda*. A few days later she meets Giovanni Battista Meneghini, a wealthy italian industrialist and opera lover.

August 2: Makes her Italian debut in the Arena at Verona as *La Gioconda* conducted by Tullio Serafin. The performances are successful enough, but Callas makes no special impression and the expected offers of further work do not materialise.

December 30 : Sings Isolde in Italian under Serafin at La Fenice in Venice and this leads to further engagements in Italy, mainly in *Turandot*.

1948

November 30: In Florence, Callas sings *Norma* for the first time an opera she will eventually perform more than any other during her career.

1949

January 19: Having just sung her first Brunhilde in *Die Walkure* eleven days earlier. Callas, at the insistance of Serafin, replaces the indisposed Margherita Carosio as Elvira in *I Puritani* at La Fenice. This is the turning point in Callas's career and the start of her involvement in rehabilition of the Italian bel canto repertoire.

April 21: Marries Meneghini in Verona and sails that night for Argentina to sing at the *Teatro Colon* in Buenos Aires.

Helps by Meneghini as both husband and manager, Callas develops her career in Italy and abroad during the next two years.

1951

December 7: Callas opens the seasons at La Scala, Milan in *I Vespri Siciliani* to great acclaim. During the next seven years La Scala will be the scene of her greatest triumphs in a wide range of roles.

1952

July 29: Callas signs a recording contract with EMI and in August makes a test recording of *Non mi dir* from *Don Giovanni*.

1953

February : First commercial recording for EMI as Lucia di Lammermoor recorded in Florence. Later in the year Callas begins a series of complete opera recordings at La Scala starting with *I Puritani* and *Cavalleria Rusticana* with Serafin, and famous *Tosca* conducted by Victor de Sabata.

1954

In a short space of time Callas loses 30 kilos and her figure changes dramaticaly. She records a further four complete operas at La Scala and her first two recital discs in London. November : She returns to the U.S.A. to sing *Norma, La Traviata* and *Lucia di Lammermoor* in Chicago.

December : She opens the season at La Scala in *La Vestale,* working for the first time with theatre and film director Luchino Visconti.

1956

October 29: Sings for the first time at the Metropolitan in New York in *Norma,* followed by *Tosca* and *Lucia*.

1957

Elsa Maxwell, the American society hostess, introduces the Meneghinis to the Greek shipping magnate Aristotile Onassis at a party in Venice.

1958

January 2: Claming illness , Callas walks out after the first act of a gala performance of *Norma* in Rome attended by the President of Italy and all Rome society. She is harshly criticised in the media.

May: At La Scala during performances of *Il Pirata* she quarrels with the general director Antonio Ghiringhelli, and decides not to appear again at La Scala while he remains in charge.

November 6: Rudolf Bing director of the Metropolitan Opera, fires Callas after failing to reach agreement on performances for the next season.

December 19: She makes a sensational debut in Paris in a gala concert at the Paris Opera. Celebrities in the audience include Onassis who begins to take interest in Callas.

1959

By this time Callas has fewer professional engagements. She and Meneghini are invited for a cruise in July on the Christina, Onassis's yacht, with several other guests including Churchill. By the end of the cruise Callas and Onassis are lovers and the Meneghini marriage is over.

1960/1961
Callas gives up the stage altogether and devotes herself to the international high life with Onassis. By 1962 she is performing only at few concerts.

1964
January: Zeffirelli persuades Callas to return to opera at Covent Garden in a memorable new production of *Tosca* that is highly praised on all counts.May : Callas appears in Paris in *Norma,* directed by Zeffirelli, in a spectatcular staging that is to be her last new production. Despite some vocal problems, the performances are succesfull overall.

1965
February: She sings nine performances of *Tosca* in Paris.March : She makes a triumphant return to the Metropolitan in New York in two performances of *Tosca.*
May: She undertakes a further series of five performances of *Norma* in Paris. She feels tired but does not want to cancel.
On May 29 she finishes Act 2 Scene I pratically in a coma. The final scene is cancelled.
July: She is scheduled to sing four performances of *Tosca* at Covent Garden. She is advised on medical grounds to withdraw but she decides to sing just one, choosing the Royal Gala on July 5. This is the final operatic preformance of her career.

1966
Callas reliquishes her American citizenship and takes Greek nationality. Thereby technically annulling her marriage to Meneghini. She expects Onassis to marry her but he does not.

1968
October 20: Onassis marries Jacqueline Kennedy, widow of assassinated U.S. president John F. Kennedy, after having cooled his relationship with Callas.

1969
June-July: Callas plays *Medea* in non operatic film of the play by Euripides directed by Pier Paolo Pasolini. It is not a commercial success.

1971/1972
Callas gives a series of Master Classes at the Juilliard School of Music in New York. She meets up again with her old colleague, the tenor Giuseppe di Stefano, and the two become close friends.

1973
Di Stefano persuades Maria Callas to undertake an extensive international recitals tour with him to raise money for medical treatment for his daughter. The tour, a personal triumph but an artistic failure, begins in Hamburg on October 25 and continues into 1974.

1974
November 11: The final concert of the tour with Di Stefano takes place in Sapporo, Japan. This is Callas's last public performance. The liaison with Di Stefano finishes.

1975
Onassis dies, following a gall blader operation. Callas is by now a virtual recluse in Paris.

1977
September16: Callas dies in Paris, but the cause of her death still remains unclear.

PHOTO CREDITS

1. Little Maria with her parents and her older sister Giacinta.
2. The first picture of Maria with her mother; Maria at school in New York in 1937 with her schoolmates.
3. Maria, her sister Jackie and a friend at Inwood Park in New York in 1934.
4. Maria with her mother at the age of 12; Young Maria at Torri wearing a swimsuit.
5. As Medea at the Teatro comunale in Florence.
6. Information unknown.
7. Callas as incomparable protagonist of Armida in Florence on april 26, 1952 (photo by Locchi).
8. One of the pictures chosen as a stamp by the Poste Italiane (government-owned postal service of Italy).
9. Maria in Athens.
10. Maria Callas in *Norma,* Paris, 1965.
11. Information unknown.
12. Medea – La Scala, Milan, 1953.
13. Anna Bolena – La Scala, Milan, 1957.
14. Maria Callas with Beniamino Gigli in Sanremo, 1954; Maria Callas as Gioconda the night of her debut on August 2, 1947, in her dressing room at the Arena, Verona, together with Lord Harewood, English nobleman who became her first fan and longlife friend, and later also biographer.
15. Together with her husband at the Lido, Venice; Maria Callas with Elisabeth Schwarzkopf.
16.. The first portrait taken in Verona in 1947 that Maria gave to her future husband as a present.
17. Information unknown.
18. *La sonnanbula* at La Scala, Milan, April 5, 1955.
19. In the role of Leonora in *Fidelio,* August 1944, at the Erode Attico Amphiteather, Athens.
20. Callas at the Opera in Rome as Norma, 1950.
21. *La vestale* at La Scala, Milan, December 7, 1954.
22. Maria in Florence.
23. Information unknown.
24. Information unknown.

Bruno Tosi, writer, journalist and music critic, as well as cultural expert and director, is well-known as the organizer of important international shows and artistic events. One of the most memorable event was the concert "Primadonna – Belcanto italiano" held in Piazza San Marco in Venice, which was broadcast all over the world with the participation of eight opera celebrities and the orchestra of the Gran Teatro La Fenice, introduced by Regina Resnik. In 1986-87 he was appointed artistic director of the Venice Carnival and since then he collaborates in the popular event every year, reviving the *Festa delle Marie* after centuries of neglect. Tosi linked his name to the myth of Maria Callas and, since 1993, he has held the largest international exhibition dedicated to the greatest opera singer of our time. He is the President of the International Association dedicated to the *La Divina* and owns the biggest collection of her memorabilia, which he will donate, together with the complete archive of documents, to the city of Venice giving birth to a permanent museum. He is also the President of the Arthur Rubenstein Association which every year awards to the most talented soloists and conductors the prize *Premio Una Vita nella Musica* which is considered equal to the Nobel Prize. For the 2009 edition, the prestigious award was bestowed on Daniel Barenboim, for 2010 to Placido Domingo, and in the previous years to such personalities as Rubinstein, Segovia, Bernstein, Rostropovich, and Mehta. He is the author of numerous biographies on performers such as Arthur Rubinstein, Renata Scotto and Aureliano Pertile. His books *Casta Diva, Giovane Callas* and *La Divina in cucina* with recipes by Maria Callas, have been huge successes and have been translated into various languages.He has received numerous international prizes and awards and he was recently nominated *Grande Ufficiale* by the President of the Italian Republic.

Printed in Mach 2010
by Gauvin Press,
Gatineau, Québec